Unencumbered

Life in Flow
Being Having a Human Experience
An Immersive Tranceformative Program
Robert "Bobby" Cobb

Executive Director
Mindful LIfe Foundation

UNENCUMBERED -- LIFE IN FLOW

First edition. April 30, 2024.

Copyright © 2024 Robert "Bobby" Cobb.

ISBN: 979-8224413256

Written by Robert "Bobby" Cobb.

Ultimacy Press
5361 Wild Cinnamon Drive
Melbourne Fl, 32940

Also By Robert "Bobby" Cobb

Books

Building the Ultimate Bank Advisor
Unleashed
The Client Centered Banker
The Richest Man in Babylon {Advisor Edition}
Momentous

Audios Programs

The 90 Day Dazzle
Enter the Zone
First Meeting Mastery
SURF ~ The Strategic Unconscious Rapport Formula
SHIP ~ Secrets of Hypnotic Influence and Persuasion
BOMB ~ Brain's Objection Mastery Blueprint
Hypnosis for Healing
Easy Hypnotic Language Patterns
Evolve - One Thought Away!

For All the Seekers
You simultaneously made this book:
Possible
&
Worthwhile

Before We Begin

Welcome to an expedition of Self-Discovery, Self Inquiry, and Self Realization. What lies ahead is not merely a book, an audio program, or a course; it is an immersive experiential journey, curated to resonate with our deepest essence. As we embark upon this odyssey, we have the liberty to choose our path, and to consume the inquiry prompts offered through various channels and media. This is not just a book—it is a multi-channel, multimedia experience, tailored to suit diverse learning preferences.

Within these pages, we'll find a blend of the written word, audio recordings, guided trancework, videos, and soon virtual masterminds—all orchestrated to guide us toward profound insights and self-realization. Whether we prefer reading, listening, watching, or engaging in virtual sessions, the essence remains the same: a journey of inner exploration and self-realization.

As we delve into this adventure, I encourage us to approach it with an open heart, mind, and spirit. Trust our intuition, for it shall serve as our compass amidst the labyrinth of thoughts and emotions. Reflect upon our initial impressions and expectations, but remain receptive to the unfolding experience. This journey isn't about acquiring knowledge; it's about realizing a new way of being—one rooted in authenticity and inner wisdom.

While the sequence of chapters suggests a linear progression, we may soon find ourself questioning the concept of linearity itself. Life seldom adheres to a predetermined order, and neither does the path of self-discovery. Embrace the fluidity of this journey, allowing ourselves to navigate its twists and turns with grace and curiosity.

Throughout this voyage, we'll encounter a variety of audio experiences, each accompanied by carefully crafted backing tracks, including binaural beats designed to enhance our immersion. These auditory elements serve as conduits for deeper introspection, guiding us into states of contemplative trance and meditative reflection.

In contrast, the written word offers a different mode of engagement—a space for deliberate contemplation and internalization. While the message remains consistent across both mediums, the delivery varies, inviting us to explore the nuances of perception and comprehension.

It's essential to recognize that there's no prescribed doctrine or set of techniques to be mastered here. Instead, I invite we to embark on a journey of self-inquiry and validation. Question everything, including the words on these pages and the voices within our mind. Seek resonance with our own lived experience, for it is within the realm of direct knowing that true wisdom resides.

Unlike conventional programs that promise external solutions to internal dilemmas, this journey begins with a fundamental truth: You are already whole and complete. There is nothing to fix, nothing to change—only layers of conditioning to shed to reveal the radiant essence of our being.

Amidst the storms of life, remember: The sun always shines, even when veiled by clouds or obscured by nightfall. Similarly, our inner light—our innate goodness and resilience—remains constant, regardless of external circumstances. Embrace this truth, and let it guide us through the darkest of nights and the stormiest of days.

So, as we stand on the threshold of this tranceformative expedition, let us embark with courage, curiosity, and an unwavering belief in the brilliance that resides within us. Together, let us illuminate the path toward self-discovery and rediscover the timeless truth: The sun is always shining, and so are we.

Unencumbered
Awakening to Flow
Introduction: How We Got Here

In December 2016, Momentous: A Tranceformative Journey to the Center of Your Authentic Self was published. This was my fourth book. It was the first book published outside of the financial services industry and the first book focused on what I called Inner Game.

After 25 years as a professional coach, both with corporations and working with individuals, I noticed that the outer game and inner game were only loosely connected, if they were connected at all.

Outer game is the way that we make our way through the outer world. Modeling excellence and "success leaving clues", are two important parts of outer game.

For the most part, these work very well. Yet having worked with some very affluent investors and some of the most successful financial advisors on the planet, I noticed that having lots of money or being able to shop without having to look at a price tag is not the key to happiness, peace, bliss, or joy.

Momentous was a treatise on what I understood at the time was the key to achieving both: to have our outer world be a reflection of our inner calm, clarity, joy, and happiness.

It was successful. When it was originally released, it trended briefly on Amazon as one of the best sellers in the psychology category.

My long-term clients gobbled it up and loved it. The feedback from them was very positive. However, it was interesting with people who were not familiar with the work and had no previous experience with coaching. The feedback was, "It's nice. It's interesting. I enjoyed it." This was not exactly what I was hoping for in what I thought was going to be a life-changing work.

It didn't take very long to figure out the difference between the two groups was the experience that had been created with my previous clients through trance work and conversational hypnosis and guided imagery, rigorously tapping into the theater of their mind powered by the most powerful special effects department on the planet: the human imagination.

Clients received an experiential understanding and an embodied realization of some of these concepts, whereas the readers were only getting the intellectual understanding. While both are helpful and a part of the whole, the embodied understanding is where the true knowing comes from.

Little did I know at the time, that my own embodied understanding and experiential knowing was about to take a dramatic and profound shift. Writing Momentous was a completely flow-inducing experience. There's a quote from the Sufi mystic poet that seems to summarize the experience of writing that book. The Hafiz quote is, "I am the hole in the flute, that Christ's breath flows through, listen to this music."

At the time of Momentous, I had been meditating for over 30 years, 22 of those years doing an advanced technique called the TM Sidhis Program. I was a Master Practitioner of NeuroLinguistic Programming {NLP} and a Certified Master Instructor of conversational hypnotherapy. With the competence that generally goes with ignorance, I was pretty sure I had it all figured out.

Then in fairly quick succession, I had two experiences that changed everything on one level, and on another level changed nothing.

Everything still seemed the same. What perceptions had shifted, understanding had deepened. Wisdom was now deeply embodied.

The first was a meditation experience, but it's not widely practiced and to my knowledge is not taught anywhere. It's something that you read about on Reddit, in meditation threads if you read deeply enough; it's called the MaHA meditation. The MaHA meditation is said to replicate what Siddhartha experienced when he sat under the banyan tree, faced the final temptations of Mara, and awakened to a self-realization experience, what some people might call enlightenment.

This process, which I don't recommend, is waking up on day one and beginning to meditate and fast. There are no technical goals to this program. Our job is not to do anything; it's rather for three days, Just BE. Drinking only water, getting up to use the bathroom, no meals, no exercise, no naps.

I didn't make it all the way. I made it about 55 hours and had to take a 45-minute nap, and then another one at 63 hours, and somewhere around 68 hours, I just fell asleep.

What I saw, which I'm not going to try to describe because I don't think it benefits us to have an intellectual understanding at this point, and I honestly have no idea if what I saw was half delusion, half grounding, half vision quest, or maybe a blend of all of the above.

I feel like I got two gifts from that experience. One relates to a quote that has always resonated from the mystical Jesuit priest Pierre Teilhard des Jardins: *"We are not human beings that have occasional spiritual experiences; rather, we are spiritual beings having a human experience."*

I know if you've been on any type of spiritual quest or consider yourself a "seeker", you have heard that phrase so much that it just now sounds like a bumper sticker. Everybody knows it, and it may have lost a bit of its charge. In fact, it may not even have any meaning for you anymore.

What is your relationship with that saying?

- Is this the first time you have read it?
- Know it by heart and love the sentiment?
- Know it well and it has lost its charge?
- See it as a prescription for life and live by it?

There is a right answer.

Somewhere in that meditation/psychedelic breathwork/fever dream/exhausted visioning. I saw it and it was so obvious. At that moment, the carefully constructed "identity" my conditioning initially built, and to which my ego later added, simply fell away. I finally stopped looking for a moment through a seeker's eyes and the elusive obvious was finally apparent.

I use this axiom now like rumble strips on the highway of life. Baby bumpers in a bowling alley as guidance to keep the ball rolling down the lane.

There's an interesting shift in this work. Initially, clients will often say, "Yeah, yeah, I get it; spiritual beings having a human experience. But there'll be the bills, fighting with my wife, my boss was a jerk, whatever it is, but yes, I get it."

This continues...it continues right up until it doesn't.

There comes that flash of insight, that aha moment. Sometimes unbelievably dramatic, and other times not so much. For many, it's not so much of an aha moment, at all. It's more like, "Oh, Now I get it," moment.

This shift is one of those little hinges that swing, some very, very big doors.

The second was the gift of perpetual meditation. Going through that long experience, I did come to realize that meditation is not something that we do. It's something that we are. Each perception, each idea, each emotion, and each feeling that we experience can be our mantra, and this is something that we'll explore in depth as we continue through the program.

The next experience occurred about three weeks later while visiting my brother and his wife. I had not been feeling particularly well, which was kind of an unusual experience for me. I'm not somebody that has a lot of aches and pains. I don't get sick very often. Which is a good thing because I'm a total wimp when I do get sick.

I was not on any medication, but I was feeling off, and when baby breaux and his wife got up one morning, they knew something was wrong.

I felt like I was meditating. I could hear them clearly. My sister-in-law commented on the fact that I drank almost half a gallon of "Green Machine" and if something was off, they came over and checked on me.

As I said, I just felt like I was meditating. I was very aware of their presence. They were asking me if I was okay. And in my head, I was responding to them. I'm saying, I'm just meditating.

Turns out my mouth wasn't moving, and they couldn't hear any of that communication. They decided to rush me off to the emergency room. I felt this was completely uncalled for and resisted, although the resistance was only occurring inside my head.

It's difficult to explain because I really did feel like I was able to communicate with my brother. He doesn't live very far from the emergency room as we're driving there. He's looking over at me, and I have kind of an out-of-body experience. I could see my body slumped down in his truck. I was looking at him from the perspective of sitting up fully. A bizarre experience to be sure. We ended up at the ER; the hospital already had the crash cart because my sister had called in advance. They admitted me into the hospital and started running tests to try to figure out what the hell was going on.

As awareness, "I" was fully present. I felt as aware as you are listening to the sound of my voice right now. However, I was non-responsive. They ran tests, and it didn't take them long to find out what the problem was. They ran my blood, and my hemoglobin level was four. This meant nothing to me the first time that I heard it, but blood for a full-grown man, hemoglobin level should be around 12.9 to 13; they start getting a little bit nervous if it gets down below 11. If it's below nine, we're supposed to go to the emergency room. Typically when we're seven, we're dead.

I was four!

I received plasma initially then whole blood. When the emergency room doc came in, I was speaking again. He said, "I can't wait to talk to the person that let his hemoglobin get down to four; he decided to come to an emergency room".

I don't remember exactly how I reacted. But judging from his reaction was taking all of this just a little bit too casually. He looked at me and he said, "You're alive for two reasons. One is the decisive action that your brother and sister-in-law took and two, whatever miracle that happened that I cannot explain."

All I knew was I felt no fear at all what was happening? There was just the realization, the understanding on a very deep level that while our bodies are not going to last forever, they are temporary. They are transient. This fact has nothing to do with us. Nothing to do with who we are.

So now, let's shift gears in a couple of interesting ways.

First, that's the last little bit of my story. Second, I'm going to suggest you don't believe the thing that "I" say. In communication, it is often helpful to have a description, but we have the ability in the human experience to turn the description into a prescription. DON'T DO THAT!

I am merely suggesting we don't take anything at face value. Try it out. Take a Test Drive.

This is easy for us to do because as we go deeper and deeper into the program, the need for understanding concepts is going to become less and less important to us. As we go through this program, we're going to be shifting from understanding things conceptually, which is the idea that we want to wrap our head around this, we want to understand it intellectually, and moving more into an experiential understanding. This is an embodied understanding, it is ***unknowing***.

Just think about just anything that we've learned. Most people have conquered gravity twice, and maybe three times in our development. The first time was as a baby. Taking those first couple of steps. I'm blessed to have both of my kid's first steps on videotape, you've seen it I'm sure they're holding on to something feeling their way into this new conceptual idea. Walking on 2 feet. "Learning" about gravity on a very visceral level, searching for balance. We may have taken a couple of steps and then may have fallen and then they take a couple more and they get there the sea legs kind or our "land legs" so to speak and then with a couple of more. We've got it. We've conquered gravity.

The same thing is true if we're riding a bike or learning how to sail a boat. It's something that we learn by doing.

When I teach hypnotherapy, the technique that we're using is called "accelerated learning". It's not really "accelerated", It's natural. We learn by doing, and there will be plenty of things for us to do.

Ultimately, where we're going is a place that's beyond words. I mean, go back to that overused phrase, when we are seeing ourselves as a human being that has occasional spiritual experiences. Think about those experiences. It can be anything. Something as simple and commonplace as the birth of a child or grandchild or seeing a child or grandchild take their very first steps. It could be a sunset, it could have been an orgasm, it could be having really, really good chocolate.

Consider this, whichever one of those may have landed for you or some other experience that's popping up in your mind. In those moments, how much do you want to talk or hear somebody else talk? We're very likely to show anybody who is crass enough to give a running commentary on this unbelievable experience. And then trying to do it later, is never going to do it justice. I intend to facilitate the co-creation of these experiences inside and finally in the way of introduction. I would simply suggest that we trust our gut, to trust the wisdom that is flowing through us 24/7.

Trust Your Inner Guru!

As we get to discussing that more definitely, one of the things that will very quickly become obvious is there are two voices within. There's the inner critic, that incessant voice for some people that is talking all the time very often saying things to us on the inside that we would never say to another human being and if anybody said those things to us might likely go up.

I know some people have a very positive and loving inner voice. So if that is you, then congratulations. Even if that is the case for you, you'll begin to notice a quiet, subtle voice begin to emerge. Even if your experience of the inner critic is more an experience of an inner cheerleader, the voice of the Inner Guru will start to emerge, as the critic/cheerleader voice starts to silence itself.

The Whispers of Wisdom are going to begin to flow out more effortlessly and obviously through us. As this occurs, look for subtle signs. Tune in and calibrate the experience. Quickly, we'll be more easily able to be recognized and that inner guidance will be easier and easier to follow.

So we can begin immediately to follow our inner guidance. And by that, I mean this program is broken down into sections. There's about 12-13 sections, I've lost count. Each section has a conceptual piece, which is a kind of food for the brain. Each one has a tranceformative imagery piece which is designed to be completely experiential.

So follow those in any way that we are guided to do it. Some people like to listen to the conceptual stuff first and then tune into the guided imagery. Other people like to reverse that order. Some people like to listen to the guided imagery audio over and over again.

*The book is designed to work through sequentially
but trust your gut,
trust your inner guidance.*

Chapter 1
"Our Perceived Reality:
Can We Believe Our Lying Eyes?"

Perceived reality is an illusion, albeit a very persistent one. - Albert Einstein

"Perception is but a mirror, not a fact. What I look upon is my state of mind reflected outward." - Ralph Waldo Emerson

In his 2019 book, "The Case Against Reality: Why Evolution Hid the Truth from Our Eyes," Professor Donald Hoffman convincingly lays out the case for the hunch that our senses are telling us something other than the truth. In reality, our senses are not optimized for truth-seeking but rather for the evolution and the survival of the species. With a mere little bit of reflection, one can bring this realization of the perceived reality into the light.

In fact, the light, as it were, is a wonderful place to start. It looks like the sun rises in the east, climbs into the sky, and then sets in the west. When we talk about it, we don't even talk about it being a perceived reality or that it appears that way. When stated with the fact "rises in the east, sets in the west," the earth feels stable and still, but science tells us that the reason for this apparent rising and setting is because we're spinning around our axis. We know at the equator it takes 24 hours for the Earth to make one revolution and we've called that a day. But what is a day?

We know that the further that we get away from the equator whether North or South depending on the time of year, our days appear to be getting longer. I live in south-central Alaska. Yesterday was April 20th, or 4/20 for those of us so inclined. Yesterday, the sun set for the last time in four months and four days. Our next true sunset is not until August 25th. We've named it a day. But is that a construct?

It certainly is a construct for the bears who will be leaving their dens after having slept for six months and begin gorging themselves on fresh leaves and bear root, which are natural laxatives, which they'll need after not doing anything in that department for the last six months.

Soon the salmon will be running and the berries will be ripening, for the Alaskan bears, a year must look like one long day, half in darkness, half in light.

What about the ocean? Once we've ever been on our ship at sea or even just stood on the beach and looked down at the horizon, we can see why people thought Columbus might fall off the edge of the Earth. It looks flat and it appears to have a quite distinctive edge.

What about the ocean itself? Depending on where we are in the world, it may appear a little brown or green or blue, it appears to have waves that have white caps, but scoop up a gallon of that ocean in a clear pickle jar and very quickly we will discover the water is colorless. So clear, we can clearly read our cell phone or our Kindle, looking through the jug.

What about the sky? Bright blue, right? Not when looked at from space. Crystal clear and colorless.

Anybody who's taken a single class in biology knows that our senses are only telling a portion of the truth. We can only see and hear roughly 4% of the Light and Sound spectrum. If we could look through the eyes of an eagle, the world would look like it's viewed through a powerful telescope.

How about the Earth? It feels stable. Yet we've already talked about making one revolution every 24 hours at the equator. It's roughly 26,000 miles which means even though we feel solid and stationary, that's not the truth because the Earth is spinning on its axis at over 1,000 miles an hour at the equator.

We know it's making its way through space as well because we are rotating around the sun. The radius of the circle that we're traveling to circumnavigate the sun has a radius of 93 million miles. Simple high school math will tell us that to make that journey in one year, we're constantly moving at more than 64,000 miles an hour.

Think about our senses for a little bit here we are reading this book, right now. Sometime in the past, I wrote it. It was digitized into ones and zeros, uploaded to the internet, and is now being re-presented on our device.

The Magic doesn't stop there. Because the light emanates from this device and it's going into our eyes. Think of the mystery of vision. Light emanates from a source, bounces off something, and goes through our pupil back to our rods and cones. Here it's digitized and sent by the optic nerve to our occipital lobe can then be rebroadcast in the theater of our mind powered by the best special effects department on the planet, human imagination.

Hearing is a similar process. A sound is a vibration. This vibration comes from a source and floats through the air in every direction. Our ear is uniquely designed to capture those waves and channel them into our ear canal. First, they tickle the cilia and bang against our eardrum. Those waves are being received, digitized, and digitally transported to our auditory cortex, which becomes the digital soundtrack for the human experience.

In reality, we have never "seen or heard" anything. All we have ever seen or heard is a digital "re-presentation" of information and energy. It's presented to us in a way that we can make sense of it.

How about our body? It seems solid right? Yet many scientists are today suggesting that our body is much more accurately thought of as a process than an object. We've been reading this chapter for approximately eight and a half minutes which means our body has made 1 billion new red blood cells. Since the amount of blood that we have in our body, for the most part, remains constant, we have therefore also eliminated roughly 1 billion red cells.

Think of the air that goes in and out of our lungs with every breath. Scientists estimate that we take in roughly about 2,000 gallons of air a day. That's roughly 570 liters per day. We know from high school biology that we're roughly about 70% fluid, not much more solid than our morning cup of coffee or tea.

I get that it doesn't look that way. And that's the point.

I began this chapter with the Einstein quote: "Reality is an illusion, albeit a very persistent one."

Consider this: How much of us is even human? We're all familiar with the terms probiotics and antibiotics. Antibiotics are specifically designed to remove the growth of all bacteria, but in most cases, killing the bad stuff, hopefully. Five minutes of an internet search will let us know that we could not survive without that bacteria. We could not digest our food.

We have microscopic parasites that are taking our dead skin that sloughs off quite easily. In fact, as we begin to notice, someplace on our body, we perceive an itch, or will be very shortly, wait for it. Now, don't fight the urge to scratch that itch. Go ahead. Doesn't it feel good?

You might not know that with *each scratch*, roughly 40,000 skin cells are being sloughed off. If we have ever had dirty fingernails, most of the dirt under those dirty fingernails is dead skin.

Look at any object. Looks solid and we can see it. However, any object, be it ourselves, a friend, an object: a chair or computer, or anything else through a very, very powerful electron microscope, and a different story unfolds. Every apparent object is made up of unique combinations of cells. Under an electron microscope as we view the cells, what we are looking at more closely resembles the solar system. Envision the solar system, the sun at the center {the nucleus}, and all of the planets {atoms}, eight or nine of them depending on whether or not we're counting Pluto, circling in a vacuum of wide-open space mostly filled with nothing at the center.

What appears to be a raging ball of fire in the sky is a mental image that we have constructed. We imagine the sun as a ball of fire that might get hotter. The closer that we get to it. We see it in our language as "hotter than the surface of the sun". But the surface of the Sun is energy inside a vacuum. The surface of the Sun has no innate heat, rather it merely emanates energy.

We have named the energy "radiation" and on that 93 million-mile journey from the Sun to the Earth, there is no transference of heat until the energy reaches the Earth's atmosphere and it has something to warm up. On a balmy, beautiful day, with the trade winds blowing softly. We can be grateful and celebrate being part of the human experience.

As we consider fully the human experience, we can appreciate what a miracle this is. The energy from the sun travels 93 million miles to the one planet in our solar system that is capable of sustaining life, and that life begins with the sunlight.

As the sunlight hits the plants, the process of photosynthesis occurs through which the plants are fed. For vegetarians, those plants are our food. For carnivores, those plants are the food of our food. Even voracious carnivores rarely eat something that doesn't have a big plant diet. One step removed.

This fact has led to the hilarious meme: "I'm not a vegetarian, but everything that I eat is," and it's funny because it's true. Those plants and or animals become us. We would not be wrong to call these whole grand goings on, a miracle.

Let's consider miracles, what is a miracle?

Some religious philosophies believe it's a very, very rare occurrence. Other philosophies look at it as a very common occurrence. Some believe that if we set the intention of getting a good spot as we are pulling into a shopping mall, we will get a really good, conveniently located parking spot.

Miracles like all the symbolic labels we give to occurrences, can mean many different things to many different people. Catholics look for one or two miracles as they seek to canonize a saint. Other philosophies teach if we are short on money and find $20 in a pair of jeans, that's a miracle. What is a miracle for you?

If we consider those two extremes, we can assume there are likely 10,000 stops between one end of that spectrum and the other. Where we are ultimately traveling is a place before words, and as we will find on this journey, words have the power to trip us up, if we ignore the fact that a miracle to we might mean something very different than what it means to another.

A big question that might be worth asking. At some point, two questions in fact, do we know the truth? Perhaps even more importantly, can we know the truth?

Werner Heisenberg, the creator of the uncertainty principle, which bears his name, suggests that until we attempt to observe it all energy is merely a probability amplitude in the field of all possibilities. Is light a photon or a wave? Could it be either or both? Can we know?

Well, as I said earlier in the introduction, I don't want you to believe any of this because I've suggested it. Test it against your experience. If you're guided to dive into some of the science, follow that guidance. We are blessed to live in a time where knowledge is abundantly available. Sadly, wisdom seems to be in somewhat short supply. Yet, on a deeper level, that apparent short supply is also an illusion.

Wisdom is speaking to us, flowing through us. Whispering the guidance of our inner guru, all day every day. As we continue this journey together, let us do so with the knowledge and the understanding of our embodied wisdom that all of the answers to all the questions that we can and might ask.

If we think about it, almost every "human" that has ever walked the earth has understood that they are part of something greater than just the finite being we call "me". Yet, how that "something greater" shows up is nearly as diverse as the perceiver's perception. I don't necessarily mean some "greater power", or "supernatural" power, some superior being, per se, but if that's the way this is showing up for us, so be it. Just go with that for now. Simultaneously, to the degree that we're able to set aside any preconceived ideas, and just use this as an opportunity to go within an experience, do that as well.

Understand what is true for you. I don't have any dogma or doctrine that I'm promoting. There is nothing that I'm asking you to believe. I will invite you to explore those beliefs, to see if some of the beliefs that you've arrived at are still true for you now. If the answer to that inquiry is yes, then by all means, keep on the path that you're on. Some have suggested this message is "anti-religion", yet I've worked with two Catholic priests, a Baptist minister, and a Methodist minister. All of whom have expressed this exploration only serves to deepen their faith.

I've worked with people in many different faiths and many people who came to me saying they had no faith at all. However, any of this is showing up for you right now is perfect.

Even if we're like, "What the heck? This guy is a loon or a preacher of pseudoscience." My role in this experience is to be a guide and to be along for the ride on our journey for now, but ultimately, my goal to the degree that there is one is merely to help us home again, to point back to our truth, to our wisdom, to our inner guidance.

Ultimately, in a now that is not yet, we may come to see ourself as a character and God's dream, a unique expression of infinite love or a perspective of awareness, or a beautiful, unique wave in the ocean of consciousness. As a species, we homo sapiens get very hung up and attached to various labels.

We have a conditioned need to be right. Nevertheless, the ability to relax and see the world through soft eyes is always available. With those soft eyes, we can see the elegance that is unfolding, the grace that is present in each moment.

As we begin to explore concepts, things, and objects, a lot of the exploration is just asking, "Is it possible for a moment to loosen some of the conditioning that we've received, and merely create a space within for new insight to flow?" Can we create the space for new intuition to enter our consciousness? Would we be open to new a-ha moments to tap us on the shoulder and show us a new perspective?

We can end this chapter back where we began, with Albert Einstein. Isn't he an interesting and unique persona? For many of us, he's nothing more than a figment of our imagination. We're told he existed historically. We have seen his picture. He left behind some papers that we can read. So there's probably a pretty good chance that he did actually happen. For most, living in the third decade of the 21st century. He is just an idea. We may, or may not, wonder as I have if half the quotes that are attributed to him actually passed his lips.

The truth of the matter is I have no idea. I've wondered how many times how many of the quotes that are attributed to Einstein may have originated from Kevin from Paducah, Kentucky. Perhaps Kevin woke up one day with a wonderful insight. thinking to himself, "Yeah, nobody's gonna believe this from Kevin. But if Einstein had asserted, OMG."

So whether it came from Albert or Kevin, a quote which seems to contain wisdom, for almost everybody, "the thinking that brought us into the situation, It's not the thinking that will get us out of the situation".

So as we continue on this journey together, I will invite you to unpack. To consider if it's worthwhile to set aside some of the limiting beliefs, debilitating thought loops, and preconceived ideas that are currently holding us back.

I'd like to leave us with a meme. A poem, six lines, three couplets.

That which we resist

will certainly persist.

What we think and

feel, we make real.

What we befriend,

we can transcend.

As we continue this exploration, I suspect we'll find as I have that what Jesus taught, what Buddha taught, what Lao Tsu, the father of Taoism, what Mohammed taught, what has been taught by every religious leader, and religious tradition, can be looked at from the perspective of the limited human mind can and can seem in conflict. Let us to consider these from another perspective.

Open our mind and our heart enough to explore from the perspective of "The Divine I am" the Divinity within us, and see from that level if they are all totally and completely in harmony with one another.

Remember, I'm not asking you to accept this view.

Rather, I'm specifically asking you to not accept this view, until you have confirmed it with your experience.

Don't believe anything that I say.

Trust your wisdom.

Trust your experience.

Trust your guidance.

Trust the whispers of wisdom that are flowing through us 24 hours a day, seven days a week 365 days a year. The wisdom we couldn't turn it off if we wanted. If we've got enough mental static going on it can seem like it's not there,

and it's not there.

It's here.

It's in the space where these words on the screen make sense to us.

This is the space we call home. This is the space where every so-called negative emotion is inviting we to return.

This is the space inside of which everything occurs.

It is the space through which everything is known.

If we have been on a seeking journey as I was, this is the 'there" we were trying to achieve.

This is an invitation to "stop trying to get there".

Because here, is all there, really is...

Chapter Two: Our Conditioned Experience

"When one realizes oneself, one realizes the true nature of the universe; the existence of apparent duality is an illusion. And when the illusion is undone, the primordial unity of one's own nature and the nature of the universe is realized or made manifest." ~ Namkhai Norbu.

I had the pleasure of attending a meeting recently, a monthly gathering I attend each month. One of the other officers of the organization recently adopted a baby, who is now about eight months old. Last Saturday, during our meeting, she brought the baby along. Everyone in attendance at that meeting could have been grandparents, and in fact, most of them were. Oohs and ahhs freely filled the air as many eagerly took turns holding the baby. Some were content simply to get close, wiggling a finger or touching a tiny toe. At one point, an attendee asked, "What is it about babies?" Another enthusiastically added, "Babies and puppies!" It's an interesting question worthy of exploration. What is it indeed?

I offered to put forth a theory, piquing the curiosity of some attendees. However, the format of the meeting, being a business gathering, didn't allow for a philosophical discussion to be added to the agenda. So, I refrained from sharing my philosophy but let those present know that I was recording this audiobook. I knew exactly where this story and explanation would fit perfectly.

What is it about babies, puppies, sunsets, or any moment that inspires or awes us? What is the common thread? As best as I can tell, these inspiring moments, whether in the presence of babies, puppies, or something else, share one commonality: they completely absorb our attention. All our awareness is 100% focused on the present moment. In this absorption, we fully accept the moment, feeling no urge to resist or interfere with the unfolding of life. Even the potential discomfort of a soiled diaper, if it were to happen, wouldn't dampen the enthusiasm of many; it would simply be a playful recognition of the situation.

Let's take this opportunity to introduce some concepts that may be new: content versus context. This distinction becomes increasingly useful as we work toward shifting our perspective to release the psychological ties that bind us to this illusory experience.

What is the content of an experience? In our meeting scenario, the content includes roughly a dozen people chatting, with a baby present who, hypothetically, may need a diaper change. Now, let's shift the context slightly. Instead of an eight-month-old baby, imagine it's a 55-year-old board member experiencing the same urge during the meeting. The content remains the same—a human answering the call of nature—but the context changes significantly.

As we move from context to context, things change because of the concepts we've attached to each specific context. These concepts are the rules we've agreed upon. Let's consider another scenario: a woman singing. If she's singing to her child, it's heartwarming. Alone in her car, it might be amusing or relatable. But singing the same song at a funeral would be deemed highly inappropriate. The context determines our reaction, shaped by the concepts we've attached to it.

Most of the rules governing our lives, whether self-imposed or imposed by others, are concepts—temporary and subject to change. The work I do often revolves around two simple yet challenging tasks: staying present in the moment and helping people realize that their limitations are mostly self-imposed. By questioning these limitations and consciously deciding which ones to keep or modify, we reclaim agency.

You're likely familiar with a parable about a family spending Thanksgiving with another family. As they prepared a ham, the chef, whoever it was, habitually cut off the end of the ham. One visitor, thinking to himself, noted that it seemed like the best part. When questioned about this, the response was, "That's just how we do it. It's a tradition like my wife does it." Intrigued, the visitor asked the wife why she cut off the end of the ham. Her response was, "I'm not sure. My mother always did it that way."

Undeterred, the visitor continued the inquiry, asking the mother, who was present, why she cut off the end of the ham. Her reply was revealing: "I have always done it that way, it's the way my momma did it. Further intrigued the visitor sets about to solve this 3 generation mystery. On to the grandmother, who was also present. To his inquiry about the tradition of cutting off the end of the ham, the grandmother responded, "I can't speak to any tradition, but I did it because my stove was too small for the whole ham."

Reflecting on this exchange, it becomes evident that what was once a practical solution for a small stove has been perpetuated without question over generations.

The reason behind the tradition had been lost, yet it persisted. As the grandmother aptly concluded, "Your guess is as good as mine" as to why this tradition endured.

In the following chapters, we'll delve deeper into the origins of our conditioning, both intellectually and experientially. By exploring our conditioning with fresh eyes and engaging in self-inquiry, we can begin to dismantle the self-imposed limitations holding us back. This process will lead us to question our conditioned beliefs, and it's a crucial step toward freeing ourselves from outdated concepts and living more authentically.

Now, let's journey back to the age of that little baby: eight months old, bright-eyed, and bushy-tailed, interacting with the world around them. Can we recall that far back? Or perhaps a better question: What is your earliest memory? For many, memories are categorized by significant events or places, often tied to early childhood experiences.

Having spoken with thousands of individuals, it's not uncommon for people to recall memories from around the age of two or three. Some memories may be even more distant, reaching back into early infancy or perhaps even claiming memories from previous lives. However, for the vast majority of us, memories before learning to speak are elusive.

As we delve deeper into our conditioning, we'll confront resistance, especially as we realize that many of the rules we've imposed on ourselves no longer make sense. This realization often triggers negative self-talk, highlighting the critical role we play as our own harshest critics.

Consider the perspective of the protagonist, the little guy in our story. What does his world look like?

Is there:

- A distinct separation of time?

- Are memories of earlier events blurred?

- Do they merge seamlessly into the present?

- How vividly does he recall moments from the day before?

- Or even earlier on the same day?

- And if memories do exist, how fully formed are they?

- Is there a clear sense of delineation, a recognition of differences between individuals, between "you" and "me," from the viewpoint of that baby?

● Did my disproportionately large head appear alien to him, or did he simply regard it as another facet of his environment, devoid of distinction from the rest of his surroundings?

Some experts posit that, prior to the onset of conditioning, babies possess a state of unconditioned awareness akin to that of a puppy—an undifferentiated, unfiltered, unconditioned perception of the world around them. When a baby gazes into our eyes, they do so with an innocence untouched by societal norms or preconceived notions. Their attention is pure, unburdened by judgment or bias, simply observing the world as it unfolds before them.

However, this pristine state of consciousness inevitably gives way to the influence of conditioning. For most children, this transition occurs between 9 and 12 months of age, though the timing may vary. During these formative months, parents often find themselves preoccupied with meeting societal benchmarks and adhering to established norms.

My wife and I experienced this firsthand when we embarked on the journey of parenthood alongside our neighbors, Nancy and Dean, who were just a few weeks ahead of us. The camaraderie offered solace amidst the uncertainty, but it also fueled our collective fixation on achieving milestones and conforming to societal expectations.

As parents, we are often acutely aware of the significance attached to our children's development. Every visit to the pediatrician becomes an opportunity to assess our parenting prowess, with growth charts and developmental milestones serving as metrics of our success—or so it seems.

In reality, these benchmarks often serve as proxies for our insecurities, reflecting our desire to excel in the role of caregiver and provider.

The quest for validation extends beyond mere physical development to encompass the realm of language acquisition. Will our child utter their first word—an eagerly anticipated milestone in every parent's journey? The competition to elicit that coveted utterance of "mama" or "dada" can become a source of both amusement and anxiety, as we eagerly await signs of our child's burgeoning linguistic abilities.

Yet, beyond the realm of language lies a more profound transformation—the emergence of individual identity.

As our children grow, they begin to recognize themselves as distinct entities, separate from their caregivers and peers. This realization marks the onset of the human domestication process, wherein societal norms and cultural expectations begin to shape their understanding of self and others.

The journey from unconditioned awareness to conditioned existence is fraught with challenges and contradictions. Our actions, attitudes, and words carry weight far beyond their immediate consequences, serving as the building blocks of our children's perception of themselves and the world around them. Yet, amidst the cacophony of societal expectations and familial influences, a fundamental misunderstanding often takes root—the belief that our feelings are a reflection of external circumstances.

In reality, our emotions are far more complex and nuanced, shaped by a myriad of internal and external factors. Yet, from a young age, we are taught to attribute our emotional states to external events, perpetuating a cycle of misunderstanding and misinterpretation. This *prime misunderstanding*, as I have come to call it, lies at the heart of much of our emotional suffering, fueling a perpetual cycle of self-doubt and insecurity.

Breaking free from this cycle requires a fundamental shift in perspective—an awakening to the true nature of our emotional experience. Rather than viewing our feelings as reflections of external circumstances, we must learn to recognize them as internal weather patterns, shaped by the interplay of thoughts, emotions, and physiological responses.

This shift in perspective is not easy, nor is it instantaneous. It requires a willingness to question deeply ingrained beliefs and assumptions and to explore the underlying patterns that shape our emotional landscape. Yet, with patience and persistence, it is possible to liberate ourselves from the grip of conditioned existence, to awaken to the true essence of our being.

In the chapters that follow, we will delve deeper into realization, exploring experiences and practices designed to facilitate this profound transformation. Through guided visualizations and reflective exercises, we will embark on a journey of self-discovery, uncovering the hidden depths of our consciousness and reclaiming our innate sense of wholeness and well-being.

Thank you for joining me on this journey of exploration and discovery. Together, let us embark on a quest for truth and understanding, reclaiming our birthright as conscious, sentient beings in a world ripe with possibility and potential. Until then, farewell.

Chapter 3:
Conditioning Our Perceived Reality,
or
It's Not Us, It's Our Conditioning

To kick off this chapter, let's delve into a couple of intriguing quotes. First, from J. Krishnamurti: "We live in a world where everything is connected. We live in a world where everything is conditioned."

Next, a quote from philosopher William James, often hailed as the father of psychology: "We're all prisoners of our minds, trapped in a reality of our own making."

And finally, words from Anais Nin: "The world is not as it is, but as we see it, and we don't see things as they are. We see things as we are."

Take a moment now to reflect on your earliest memory. Feel free to pause the recording if you need time to reach back into your past. What is the oldest memory you can recall? Picture yourself in that memory—what shoes are you wearing, and what surrounds you? How old are you in this recollection?

For most people, the earliest memories typically date back to around ages four to six, though some may recall events from ages seven to nine, and a few might even remember moments from as young as two or three. Consider your own earliest memory now, as we'll revisit this later in a guided contemplation.

Many struggle to recall events predating their ability to speak. There's compelling scientific evidence suggesting a close correlation between our capacity to form long-term memories and our brain's language processing abilities. One study in the Journal of Neuroscience found a significant link between the two. Another study, published in the Journal of Developmental Science in 2012, revealed that infants exposed to richer language environments tend to develop better memory skills, with some showing memory capabilities as early as 14 months old.

So, what's happening during this developmental phase? Several theories abound, but two prominent ones suggest that without language, memories may not be encoded into long-term storage, or that although the memories exist, our inability to articulate them linguistically hinders their retrieval. Personal experiences, like regressions under hypnosis, lend some credence to these ideas. People often express memories using the vocabulary and vocal tones of the age they recall.

Ongoing research continues to explore these theories, but in the end, it's an internal journey. The question remains: What do we believe?

To help you get concrete on what you think, I want to run a little thought experiment with you to demonstrate one thing, and that is the fact that our memory is very malleable. The way that we remember things changes dramatically as new information is added to the mix. It's one of the reasons that in hypnosis, one of our foundational ideas is: that it's never too late to go back and have a good childhood.

I had a client not too long ago who wanted to go back and explore some daddy issues. He was conceived when his dad was 15 and his mom was 14. This was in the 50s, and the parents were Catholic, so the baby was going to term. There simply were no other options back then.

We regressed him back early enough in his life that he was still sleeping in a crib, wearing diapers when he took his nap in a crib, so call it two, two and a half, three years old, or something like that, and just had a look at his dad and interacted with his dad from that standpoint.

Nothing came clear around that initially, so in the trance, we had him go into his dad's experience and feel what his dad was feeling, see what his dad was seeing, and hear what his dad was hearing.

There was a giant aha moment as a result of that. The son, who at this point was in his 60s, realized that his dad back then was 17 or 18 years old. He was a young kid who did a kind of exceptional thing, he married his mom...and they're still married today.

I asked the client to experience what his dad was experiencing, and what he experienced in the trance work was that his dad was extremely fearful. He had no idea which end was up. He was trying to figure out how to make a living, complete his school, be a good husband, be a good dad, and do all of that stuff, and it was just overwhelming. Based on this state of nearly constantly struggling, his dad occasionally lashed out.

Probably more often than the dad would have liked to react, certainly more often than the baby version of my client would have liked, in retrospect. However, in that moment when he saw:

"Oh, my God, my dad was just a kid,

and he was stressed out,

and he was scared,

and he was trying to make ends meet,

and he had the obligations of his own,

parents and his in-laws to deal with...

These all came in rapid succession during the trance work, and then...

The client realized his dad, with all those concerns on his shoulders, dared to do the right thing.

The realization hit him so hard that he had difficulty catching his breath.

The Perspective Shifted

Of course, he lashed out;

Of course, he acted through stress.

In that moment for the client, everything changed. Suddenly, all of the conditioned ideas that he had had about his dad and their interaction and their relationship with each other just fell away.

It was a beautiful thing to witness. Over a very short period, and by short, I mean just a couple of minutes, we could see him integrating this new bit of knowledge, rewriting his timeline, and looking at his relationship with his mom and his dad in a completely new and different light.

I'd like you to recall if what I'm about to describe brings a situation to mind. It can be one that you've lived through, or you may know a friend and be able to call this imagery to mind.

Think of a good friend who begins dating somebody that they think might be "the one". There's something about this person that just creeps you out from the word go. It might be something that you can't quite put your finger on, but there's a sense that this isn't going to work out.

Maybe you struggle with the idea of, "Do I say something to my good friend, or is that just going to be throwing a wet blanket on this ember of a flame that may be starting to ignite within your good friend?"

Many people have been through a situation where they decided to keep their mouth shut, and perhaps, even as things went on for a while, their idea of this person began to change.

Whatever that little inkling was, something seemed just a little bit off, maybe just kind of fades into the distance. It just fades from memory. Perhaps you've even thought to yourself, "You know, why didn't I like this person when I first met them, but I was wrong about them?"

Now, you probably know where this is going. Somewhere down the road, this person just does something awful to our friend—lies about something critical, or maybe cheats on them, has an affair, or does something that sloppily gets this person in trouble, even though that's an unintended consequence of the action.

Now, the entire timeline of the relationship of this couple starts to be rewritten in our mind. Things that you filtered out along the way suddenly are called back into the forefront again. And it's like now you're just looking for things that are reaffirming that initial gut reaction that you had a moment ago.

Think how quickly the way that you think of this person can change in one direction or another. That initial change of admitting or coming to the conclusion rather than that you were wrong about this person. In the beginning, it may take a little bit longer, but if all of a sudden they do something that recalls back that initial gut reaction, that part of the timeline, that little chunk of memory is rewritten very, very quickly.

For most people, the earliest memories that they can recall are going to be somewhere around four, five, or six years old. As we get a little older in life, what's happened before that, is a blur. We probably can't remember our childhood in the first year and a half or two years. We may have to think of a niece or nephew, child, grandchild, or a friend's baby. We've been around babies at some point in our life.

Think about the way that they make their way through the world: pure curiosity, pure beginner's mind, pure exploration, no judgment, no expectations, no preconceived ideas. Pre-language, think about how a baby is.

If you've ever seen them with a piece of paper, they want to experience that in every way possible. They stick it in their mouth to taste it, they rub it up against their face to see how it feels, crinkle it so that they can hear the different sounds it's making and the different ways that they manipulate the page, they look at it, they test its tensile strength by trying to tear it apart or crumple it up.

They might try to tear it, then perhaps get a little frustrated and cry, and then fall and start to laugh all over again. Babies, by their very nature, are magnetically attractive. People come and see the baby, and they just want to get near it. Impetus will tell you that they are some of the best hypnotists in the world because the moment that an adult who has had a baby or a baby in their life that they're close to comes in contact with another baby, it's instant trance—we are connected to pure being, pure consciousness, pure awareness.

Unconditioned, they look with the same love that a little puppy does. And being in that space for even just a couple of minutes is a powerful pattern interrupt.

Somewhere along the way, as we make oohs and ahhs and start to vocalize and play around a little bit with our vocal cords, our parents begin a little contest to see what's going to be our first word. Wouldn't it be "mom"? Will it be "daddy"? It's like the parental pride sweepstakes—an absolutely silly game that no one can resist playing. Regardless of which parent wins the sweepstakes, prizes bragging rights even! "She learned me first".

What happens next? The baby very quickly learns the other parent's label and the names of any siblings that they may have and their name. "My name is Mommy, you are Bobby." And we are asked to adopt what I believe is a conditioned belief that we're separate. Now that in and of itself is no big deal. The odds are pretty good that whatever age you are, you still believe this. Perhaps, it's a belief that you've already begun to let go of a bit. Maybe, you've already let it go altogether. Many, many people go through their entire lives operating happily and effectively with this belief foremost in their minds in many cases.

Now, if we Google "separation anxiety," we're going to find out that that normally occurs in kids between 18 and 24 months of age, although it can also occur later. What else is going on there? We've been living and operating under the assumption that this is all a big wonderful bubble of exploration and curiosity. And it's all awesome, and I'm part of it all. I've got my place in it.

Then we start to learn that this person whose eyes we've been looking into can't look into our own without a mirror. This person whose eyes we've been looking into is a whole different person called Mama, and sometimes she's here and sometimes she's not.

If we Google this, entering normally between 18 and 24 months can also occur later. Then it says it is a normal and healthy part of development. Children learn to differentiate between themselves and their caregivers and develop a sense of autonomy. "Normal and healthy". Well, we'll see about them. Interesting words, aren't they? We'll come back to those.

So once we have language, now the idea of separation can be introduced into the mix, and the real conditioning can start to happen. And here's how it normally goes: If you have a good parent who's had some parenting one-on-one training, they will not tell you that you make me mad at you. They will tell you, "Your actions make me mad. I love you, but your actions make me mad." So unpack that just a little bit. What has to be true for that statement to be true? It's got to be that I can make you feel a certain way. I could make you feel happy. I could make you feel sad. And wouldn't it be oh so wonderful if we had that power to be able to go up to somebody and say, "You feel happy now"? I mean, think about it for just a little bit. If you're not in a good mood, you're in the office, and you're having just a crummy day, and down the hallway comes Professor positive. Seems like every office has got one, and they see you down, and they say, "Why the long face, their partner? You know, the world is just a projection of what you're feeling.

Fake it until you make it." Does that ever work? And the truth of the matter is, yeah, it does. Sometimes.

Sometimes. A nice, kind word from somebody can lift us. They can help to release that cloud. But can we say it's causative? And by that, I mean, can we say that these words, handed to a person who is down, will reliably, repeatedly, and sustainably deliver that result? Time and time again? Like most people would agree, absolutely not. When I ask people this, they normally either say that never happens, or "Sometimes it does, but it's pretty rare." More often than not, we might consider it the exception that proves the rule that we don't have a magic ability to change the way that somebody else is experiencing life on the inside. As best we can say we can influence it, but certainly can't control it. And yet, that is the logical conclusion of that little bit of communication. If they accept that in, and if we accept that in, what you did makes me feel sad inside, then we are presuming that we do have the ability, not just to influence but really to control how somebody else is feeling on the inside. Now here's the cool thing.

This is a relatively recent phenomenon, the result of an idea that some people have called Enlightened Parenting, where we are not going to criticize the person. Not even going to comment on the behavior, but rather to discuss how that makes us feel. I think if we look into this, we'll see that this is an unintended consequence of an okay idea. We know, a couple of generations ago, it was very common that we would just criticize our children and tell them, "You're bad" or "What's the matter with you, Mark? Can't you get along? Why are you an evil little kid?" So child psychologists came up with the understanding that if you do that repeatedly, to somebody who is a beautiful, young, developing, future, brilliant mind, but if you're throwing that into a young developing mind over and over again, particularly when you're doing it at the level of identity, you are likely installing some pretty debilitating thought loops and some mental models that are just in no way useful. So to correct that, we swung the pendulum completely to the opposite end of the arc, solving one problem while simultaneously creating two new ones.

First, we are creating this artificial super importance to our feelings. There's a quote that's been around for a while that states, "Facts don't care about our feelings." Thirty or forty years ago, that was considered common sense. In the 2020s, it's considered hate speech. It used to be that if we didn't like something that we saw or heard the most common and most likely response was, let's vote with our feet. Go ahead and leave, change the channel if it's not your particular flavor of ice cream, or if it was something that you disagreed with. Make your case, speak up, let's have a conversation. Today, it's routine that if somebody visits a college campus, and wants kind of the citadels of free speech the school feels obligated to provide a safe place including counseling for anybody who may be offended by the fact that somebody with a contrary opinion has been invited onto the campus. The importance of our feelings has just been blown completely out of proportion.

But that's the smaller of the two problems and the other one is both more pernicious and more pervasive. It is all over the place and that is installed at a much, much earlier age, the belief, that mistaken belief that our feelings are telling us about our circumstances, and they never, ever are not once, but it's a very pervasive belief. I would go so far as to say almost everyone we know holds that belief, the belief being our feelings are telling us about our circumstances.

And I can almost hear you pushing back thinking well, sometimes they are. And here again, don't believe me because I'm telling you; in a moment, I'm going to experientially show you if there's any confusion as to what I'm talking about. Here's a little experiment that we can run with our friends. And that simply is when the next time you see one of them that looks different, just comment on the fact that they look different in whatever way that is. I mean, be very specific. "Wow, you look up, you look super happy" or "Wow, you look like you just got hit with some bad news" or "You know, you look a little bit off today."

Whatever it is, and just see what the response is. When we get a response, just check and see, if they have credited whatever it is that they're feeling with an external object of some sort. So if they're up, are they saying "Some man just had a financial windfall" or "I got a bit of good news" or "I got a promotion" or "I met the one"? If they're down, are they saying "My boss is an asshole" "Where I'm having trouble at home" or "My car keeps breaking down" or "I think I'm gonna get fired"?

I'm gonna get fired.

Some external circumstances that are showing us the linguistic structure of their belief that the cause for the way that they're feeling is something external to them. And with that belief, it's very smart. It makes common sense. It is logical and rational to assume that our feelings are telling us about our circumstances. And let us for this conversation, just assume that that is a given. It looks as if that is the cause of our internal experience; our external circumstances are the cause. It's just conceded that it looks that way.

Let's dig a little bit deeper. Let's have a moment of self-reflection, a little self-exploration, a little inquiry to see if that's actually what's going on. Because I want to submit to you it's an illusion, and I'm going to attempt to prove it to you experientially so that you will not have just an intellectual understanding; you'll have that as well. We'll also have an embodied knowing that is an illusion. And amusing the way that a magician uses the illusion of magician can stand in front of you and seemingly out of midair, can make a coin up here can make a coin vanish, seemingly offering you free choice. They can force you to select a card of their choosing, but it doesn't look like that's what's going on. Our eyes are telling one story, intellectually we understand that we're not making the card out of thin air manifesting the card out of thin air, but it does look exactly that way.

So we need to get down to the essence of what's happening. So what are we talking about? Essence? Well, let's talk about water. We all know the formula for water if we wanted to make two molecules of hydrogen, and one molecule of oxygen, bind them together. And then we have water. That is the essence of water. If we put a little lemon in there, if we put a little cucumber in there, we still have the essence of water. And we have this additional flavor. That's been added to the mix as well. Now, water comes in three different forms. It can be a solid, in the case of an iceberg or an ice cube. It can be a liquid in the case of a glass of water, or above 212 degrees, it can be steam, but in any three of those manifestations. What is the deep essence of water whether it's a solid, a liquid, or a gas to an ingredient to molecule hydrogen, two hydrogen molecules, and one oxygen molecule only the temperature has anything to do with how that's going to show up. But at its core at its essence. It's the same thing, regardless of how it happens to be manifesting in the moment. Now, here's another illusion.

What is a mirage? If we're out in the desert and we're walking to the horizon, or if we're driving, we can look out on the horizon, we can see a mirage that looks like an oasis. Out there in the desert. Everything's dry. Everything is hot, but we look off into the horizon. And there's a body of water in the distance. We can see it right with our own eyes. Right.

Intellectually, we have come to understand that that's an illusion. And the way that we know that is an illusion is by exploring the essential ingredients of the mirage. There is no water in a mirage, probably hydrogen, probably oxygen, but they're not combining in such a way that they're forming. Water. What is the essence of the Mirage?

Also two ingredients. It requires heat and it requires light. And those two essential ingredients create the illusion that our senses are telling us as a body of water just out there, just shy of the horizon. Eight miles and we'll be at the water. Of course, we travel those eight miles and the Mirage is typically still out there. Right before the horizon eight miles ahead.

Let's look at a different example. I don't know if you've ever in our life been a commuter that has to travel a distance in a vehicle and you're traveling to a place where there's relatively kind of heavy traffic where there's the likelihood that there's going to be traffic jams along the way and slowdowns for one reason or another, and you know one of the banes of the existence of the commuter is the traffic tram along the way.

I want you to look at the essence of the traffic jam. What's involved with that? Well, typically wherever it is that you're commuting, you're going to be traveling more or less the same road in the same car, surrounded by more or less the same people going in the same direction and more or less the same time.

If you can recall that memory from experience, I would just like you to think about getting cut off. We're driving on here comes somebody; they pull around here, they cut in traffic's heavy so they gotta have their but have their cars sticking out in the other lane and wait for the traffic to move far ahead enough for them to squeeze in but they got the jump on you, you know they're in front of you and you can proceed without hitting them so they're gonna wedge themselves one car ahead of where they would have been otherwise in front of you.

How do you react to that? We may have a reflexive response that you know, I would be pissed off or I would be okay with it. I would just allow them to be in, but the real experience if you dive into it is all of those possibilities are within you. It's not a cause-and-effect relationship.

It's not that they pulled in front of us and therefore we're pissed off or therefore we're gracious, or therefore we're irritated or whatever the label that we may put on that description of the moment maybe instead of being a cause and effect the way that it looks. It's a stimulus and a response.

So the stimulus is the core cutting in front of us. And what's the response? Well, it could be a lot of things I posted a meme on Facebook earlier:

me: be kind you never know what somebody else is going through.

also me: nice turn signal fuckface.

For everyone that I've ever asked, both of those responses are in there. Now for many people, the latter response will never be uttered yet. It's still there.

That's the very reason that we can know somebody who's very prim and proper, very devout, but occasionally will laugh at a very inappropriate, very dirty joke because laughter is an involuntary response. They're touching something that is in us through the comedy in a very visceral way and out comes the laugh.

So to continue the parable of the commuter, the metaphor of the commuter, we can imagine if we are that commuter that there may be one week where we're driving to work. Traffic is slow. It's backed up for whatever reason. We're engrossed at the moment; we're listening to a wonderful piece of music, or maybe a fascinating podcast, or maybe we're just lost in thought, but we're just really experiencing a very peaceful Zen-like moment. That person slips in front of us and cuts us off. What is the likelihood that we may give "we never know what else somebody else is going through" responses? It has increased significantly, right?

The following week, we can be driving, the same person, the same car traveling down the same road, the same time surrounded by more or less the same people. But somebody cuts us off and we might reach under our seat and pull out a pistol and blow out a rear tire? A verified road rage kind of incident.

We go back to that quote that I started this chapter off by Anais Nin, "The world is not as it is, but as we see it. And we don't see things as they are. We see things as we are".

Now the cool thing is, this is not a new idea. In the Talmud, they say almost the exact same thing. We see things not as they are, we see them as we are. I mean, this is ancient, ancient Old Testament-type teaching.

Stephen Covey said, "We don't see the world as it is; we see the world as we have been conditioned to see it."

Ralph Waldo Emerson said, "We see the world through our own limited perception or needs."

Henry David Thoreau said, "The world is a canvas for our imagination. We paint our own reality."

We get this, yes? I mean, we can intellectually all understand this concept.

Here's my invitation. As we continue through this program, as we do the guided visualizations that we're going to do at the end of each chapter, I want to invite you to sit with this idea on a much deeper level through the transport that we'll be doing together.

I want to help you understand this concept not just on the intellectual level; we will still get it there. But I want it to be our embodied understanding, an unknowing that is baked into every fiber of our being.

So I'm going to close this chapter out here. We'll move directly into the guided hypnotic experience, the guided visualization, to help us move into an area where this is not just something that we conceptually understand because we can conceptually understand a bumper sticker. But if we only conceptually understand a bumper sticker; it has little to no impact or meaning in our lives and our relationship with the human experience.

So when you're ready, not driving, someplace that you can relax and take a few deep breaths and probably close your eyes. It's more comfortable for most people. If they're doing that. We can head on over to the next recording, the audio experience for chapter number three.

We will see you there. Ciao for now.

Chapter 4

Life Only Unfolds One Way: Divinely.

Every moment is a masterpiece for those with the eyes to see and the ears to hear.

Two quotes to begin this chapter: the first one from the Buddhist monk Thich Nhat Hanh, "Do not chase the past. Do not lose yourself in the future. The past no longer is. The future has not yet come. Looking deeply at life as it is in the very here and now, the practitioner dwells in stability and freedom."

And from the Dalai Lama, "There is no need for temples, no need for complicated philosophies. My brain and my heart are my temples; my philosophy is kindness."

I have a small group of R&D people who are listening along to this book, going through these exercises, and doing these meditations as a sort of research and development group. I have shared this message for years, and many people have gone through the program we are virtually experiencing in this book. However, I've never taught it in a one-to-many format, and there's a completely different skill set involved in that.

One-to-one has the advantage that I can address whatever is occurring in the individual specifically. When a question arises, I encourage them to ask it. If something doesn't sit right, I encourage them to push back. This is an experience, an exploration, an adventure.

So, part of this project for me is learning the new skill set of sharing this message that I have mastered in a one-to-one setting.

Over 200 people have gone through the immersion now, and all but about 11 have had the desired outcome of seeing things differently and feeling unencumbered by the worn-out mental models, limiting beliefs, and the hypnosis of social conditioning that have filtered their experience for many years.

During both the one-to-one sessions and with some of the R&D people who are along for the ride, a common question arises: are we talking about enlightenment or something else?

The reason it's a question is enlightenment; it's a word I rarely, if ever, use.

I've heard others answer the question about enlightenment differently. Two people I have a decent relationship with gave two very different answers.

The first person's approach resonated with me. He didn't like to use the word enlightenment because he felt it could trap the ego. The moment someone claims to be enlightened, a series of expectations and behaviors pile on, leading to skepticism from others. The rational mind quickly tries to categorize behaviors associated with enlightenment, creating a checklist to assess someone's alignment with the concept. It also seems to be the ultimate gig for the ego.

The second version of answering the enlightenment question comes from Byron Katie. When asked if she considers herself enlightened, her response was direct. She said, "Well, I've seen the source of suffering, so I'm going to say yes." I appreciate this answer because it simplifies the complex experience of "enlightenment". Unpacks it and makes it ordinary and accessible.

Regardless of what we call it, the experience of waking up to our true nature and seeing life as it is can be profound or subtle, completely life-altering, or just a shift in perspective.

Some may experience a dramatic transformation akin to the biblical story of Saul becoming St. Paul on the road to Damascus. Others may have a more subtle realization, like Neo in The Matrix after taking the red pill. Regardless, it's about seeing things differently and feeling liberated from the constraints imposed by social conditioning.

Most people mistakenly believe that enlightenment involves changing their behavior, purifying their thoughts, and emulating an idealized image of an enlightened being. However, this approach only reinforces the ego's desire to play a role. The truth is, that "enlightenment" is not about adding more to ourselves but realizing that we are already complete. Our inherent qualities like resilience, compassion, and creativity are not something to be achieved but are part of our essence.

Our biggest challenges on this journey are twofold: reality is indescribable, and our conditioned beliefs about reality hinder our understanding. Reality is ineffable, beyond words. Our attempts to conceptualize it often lead to oversimplified and inaccurate models. Our beliefs about ourselves and the world are shaped by early-age conditioning, creating a distorted narrative that obscures the truth of our experience. To awaken from this dream of self-importance, we must suspend our conditioned beliefs and directly perceive the actuality of our situation, as it is.

Many people labor under the mistaken belief that enlightenment entails a meticulous overhaul of our actions, an amplification of compassion, a quest to untangle confusion, and a purification of karma. This misconception leads them to believe that by adhering to the behaviors they associate with enlightened beings—thinking positively, performing altruistic acts, and striving for an imagined state of perfection—they will attain enlightenment. However, our first friend's answer above saw this pursuit as a potential trap, recognizing it as the ego's ultimate role-playing game.

The desire to emulate the behavior of enlightened beings can become a mask for the ego, a guise it eagerly dons. However, the truth is far simpler: enlightenment, whether labeled as such or referred to by various spiritual terms, ultimately points to the innate state of Being itself. It is not something to strive for through years of meditation or adherence to rigid practices; rather, it is a realization that our essential nature is already enlightened.

As Pierre Teilhard de Chardin aptly put it, we are not human beings having occasionally spiritual experiences rather, we are spiritual beings having a human experience. This perspective shift unveils the truth that our being requires no purification or enhancement—it is already complete. Traits like resilience, compassion, creativity, and intuition are not acquired through external efforts but are inherent aspects of our being, installed at the factory, by the manufacturer, part of the original equipment.

The veil of societal conditioning obscures this truth, leading us to believe that happiness and enlightenment can be attained through external means—a formulaic approach perpetuated by marketing and societal norms. However, the realization dawns that true enlightenment comes not from striving to become someone else, but from embracing and realizing the inherent perfection of Our Being.

The truth of our situation is inconceivable. Our finite minds cannot grasp the infinite nature of reality. While reality is indescribable, it is directly knowable through experience. Our Orienting Hypnotic Meditations allow us to bypass linguistic barriers and experience reality as it is. We are already intimately connected to reality; we just need to recognize it.

Our journey involves overcoming our conditioned beliefs and directly perceiving the ineffable nature of reality. It's a process of awakening from the dream of self-importance and realizing our inherent completeness. As we explore these concepts further, we open ourselves to the possibility of true understanding and liberation.

As a result of these conditioned beliefs, most of us live in a fantasy world, ignoring any experiences that don't fit into our oversimplified beliefs. We navigate through life like sleepwalkers, oblivious to the true nature of our existence. However, some individuals become disenchanted with their stories, either because they realize their pursuit of material success hasn't brought them happiness or because their lives haven't unfolded as expected.

To awaken from this dream of self-importance, we must suspend our conditioned beliefs and directly perceive the actuality of our situation. This requires a willingness to question our assumptions and examine our experience without preconceived notions. Through guided awareness meditations and introspection, we can begin to unravel the layers of conditioning that obscure the truth. As we do so, we open ourselves to the possibility of genuine understanding and liberation.

In essence, our journey is about recognizing the limitations of our conditioned beliefs and embracing the boundless potential of direct experience. It's a process of awakening to the ineffable reality that lies beyond words and concepts—a reality that we are already intimately connected to. As we continue on this journey, we deepen our understanding of ourselves and the world, ultimately finding freedom from the constraints of social conditioning and self-imposed limitations.

In this state of delusion, mistaking our conceptualized version of reality for the actuality. We navigate through life like sleepwalkers, unaware of the true nature of our existence. Awakening from this delusion requires us to suspend our conditioned beliefs and directly perceive the actuality of our situation.

To overcome these hindrances, we must cultivate a willingness to question our assumptions and examine our experience without preconceived notions. Guided awareness meditations offer us a powerful tool for bypassing the limitations of language and thought and experiencing reality as it is.

Through these meditations, we can glimpse the ineffable nature of reality and begin to unravel the layers of conditioning that obscure the truth. As we deepen our understanding of ourselves and the world, we open ourselves to the possibility of genuine liberation from the constraints of social conditioning and self-imposed limitations.

In essence, our journey is one of awakening to the inconceivable reality that lies beyond the limitations of our finite minds. It is a journey of letting go of our conditioned beliefs and embracing the boundless potential of direct experience. As we continue on this journey, we deepen our understanding of ourselves and the world, ultimately finding freedom from the constraints of social conditioning and self-imposed limitations.

This journey is not without its challenges, but it offers the promise of true liberation and understanding. As we continue to explore the depths of our being and the nature of reality, we open ourselves to the possibility of profound transformation and awakening.

We come to recognize life's simplicity and its inherent beauty. These assumptions often stem from teachings or the examples we've absorbed from our surroundings, almost as if through osmosis—be it from our families or our immediate culture. We adopt these notions as truths, integrating them into the framework of our belief systems, the facade we present to the world. We then build upon them, using them as the foundation for further notions about ourselves and our circumstances.

These ideas become ingrained in consciousness, fueled by the emotional investment we have in certain beliefs. For instance, the belief in separation from the universe, vulnerability, or neediness. We construct intricate narratives around these fundamental beliefs, crafting elaborate soap operas with ourselves as the central characters. These dramas are filled with imagined hopes, fears, dangers, and rewards, all fueled by self-importance and heightened emotional responses.

Consequently, many of us find ourselves lost in a fantasy world, disregarding any experiences that don't align with our oversimplified self-referential beliefs. We navigate through life like zombies, unaware of the reality beyond our internal dreamscapes. So, we may be asking, "How do I awaken from this internally constructed dream of self-importance, rooted in fantasy?"

Can we perceive the potency of conditioning? Can our awareness grasp its grip? Then, what is to be done? The fortunate truth unveils that we all possess an intimate connection to reality, an innate familiarity that has never waned. We are, in essence, manifestations of reality itself. Thus, our task is to simply acknowledge the actuality of our existence.

The primary obstacle we encounter on this journey lies in our conditioned inclination to adhere to our fabricated narratives, obscuring the genuine reality of our experience. To truly apprehend our situation, we must be willing to momentarily suspend our allegiance to these ingrained beliefs and behold the unadulterated truth. Once this shift occurs, further exploration into the depths of our being becomes more accessible. Yet, it necessitates interrupting the conditioned responses that cloak our perception, allowing the pristine essence of reality to emerge from beneath the layers of conceptual constructs.

Typically, only those who have grown somewhat disillusioned with their personal narrative show any inclination toward this inquiry. Such disillusionment often arises for two transient reasons.

Firstly, there are those of the peak performer types, adept at setting and achieving goals, driven by the belief that accumulation and achievement lead to lasting fulfillment—the "he who dies with the most toys wins" philosophy. They tirelessly pursue material acquisition, convinced that it will ultimately yield happiness. After a time, when all the goals have been realized except happiness, they reach the inevitable conclusion, "I must be missing something".

Alternatively, some find themselves disenchanted simply because their life story fails to unfold as envisioned. They come to realize that the inner disquiet they experience isn't solely a product of external circumstances but stems from a deeper, more profound source. Could it be wisdom calling them home again, in the only way it can get the message through? By making her miserable?

The truth of our existence eludes conceptual grasp. Deliberately employing the term "inconceivable," reminiscent of The Princess Bride's playful treatment of the word, I underline its profundity. It surpasses verbal expression, transcending description, for it is not something we merely apprehend; we are inseparable from it, utterly and completely.

This ineffable nature perpetuates its enigmatic quality. Consider this:

If reality were within the realm of conception or description, those who grasp it would effortlessly convey it to others, dispelling their confusion. Yet, reality defies such simplistic comprehension.

In discussions of hypnosis, we often contrast the conscious mind with the subconscious or unconscious mind, likening it to an iceberg, with a mere fraction visible above the surface, while the vast majority remains submerged, directing our responses and actions from the depths. This metaphor aptly captures much of the human experience, yet, in the context of our exploration, it falls short.

As I've mentioned before, Einstein nailed it with his quote: "The rational mind is a faithful servant, and the intuitive mind is a sacred gift", but here's the kicker: "We're living in a world where we worship the servant and have forgotten the gift".

This perfectly sums up what we've been getting at here.

In our exploration, let's dive into the heart of what's being said. It's helpful to split things into two: our everyday, limited thinking and the vast, Infinite mind that's the source of everything. This bigger mind? It's beyond birth and death – it's always there.

When we think about it, reality is beyond words or ideas. It's like trying to fit an ocean into a teacup. Our reality is always open-ended and personal – there's no fixed rulebook.

Our minds want to make sense of it all by creating simple, stable stories. But these stories just get in the way of seeing things as they really are.

That's where this conversation and the accompanying audio come in handy. They let us directly experience reality without all the mental chatter. Rupert Spira talks about us "as Awareness". The Infinite and Eternal space inside of which everything occurs. Through which, everything is known. Of which, everything is made.

Let's dive into that deeper understanding and let go of the need for words to explain everything.

In our current state, we find ourselves within the expanse of infinity, a realm that defies confinement by fixed or objective conditions. This truth eludes rational categorization and finite comprehension. Attempting to encapsulate the infinite with our finite minds is akin to grasping at shadows. The very essence of our reality is boundless, subjective, and beyond the grasp of finite definitions.

It becomes evident that our finite faculties are inadequate to apprehend the infinite. This limitation lies at the heart of our quest for understanding. Yet, our linguistic constructs and conceptual frameworks, though useful in navigating our world, inevitably fall short when faced with the boundless expanse of truth.

In our pursuit of security and stability, we fabricate simplified models of reality, seeking comfort amidst the perceived chaos. However, these constructs, however comforting they may seem, only serve to veil the true nature of our existence. Our manufactured beliefs become barriers to perceiving reality as it truly is: ineffable yet directly accessible to the intuitive knowing that transcends mere description.

Therefore, it is through direct experience, unencumbered by the limitations of language and concept, that we come to apprehend the inherent truth of our being. This truth, though indescribable, is nonetheless palpable to the open heart and receptive mind.

Consider this: throughout our lives, we've never known or experienced anything other than reality itself. Reflect on it deeply—how could we possibly experience something unreal? What substance would it be composed of? How would it manifest within our awareness?

If something arises in our experience, it must inherently be of the essence of reality. Even the skeptic may argue that our interpretation of what arises in consciousness could be flawed. Yet, this questioning does not render the experienced phenomena unreal; rather, it underscores the profound mystery and depth of our perception.

Experience can be understood as a ceaselessly shifting interplay of energies, forever new and unfamiliar, emerging within the field of consciousness. What these energies are made of, or what triggers their arising and passing away, remains a fundamental enigma. They emerge spontaneously within the space of awareness, consciousness, or being, or what some may term as the Holy Spirit or God's infinite love.

By grasping this, we come to recognize consciousness as not just the passive backdrop of experience, but the very mechanism through which experience unfolds. This insight reveals that consciousness is both the medium and the content of reality, and any attempt at distinction between the two is arbitrary.

These energies never appear independently; they are intricately interwoven. Yet, due to our conditioned perspective, we often feel compelled to categorize experiences into distinct domains based on their apparent qualities—sight, touch, smell, taste, hearing, and even thought, emotion, and intuition, if we delve deeper into the spectrum of human perception.

We might even delve into the realm of what some might dismiss as "hippy-dippy" or "woo-woo" philosophy, speaking of vibrations and vibes. Yet, within these frameworks, the flow of energy gives rise to the illusion of separate and individual objects, leading us astray from the underlying unity of existence.

I like thinking of our experience like being in a movie theater. We know, in the theater of consciousness, we've got this energy, this light of being that's like the power behind the projector. It shines on the screen of awareness, bringing to life all sorts of stories. Some days it's a romance, other days a comedy, or maybe an action-packed adventure, a spy thriller, or even a scary horror flick. It's like all these possibilities playing out on the screen.

Think back to when you were really into a movie, lost in the story. You probably weren't even aware that it was all happening on the screen, right? Well, that's kinda like us with our true self. We're like the movie theater itself, and the stories are just passing through, flickering for a while, and then fading away.

Just like when a movie ends and the screen goes black, if we stick around through the credits, eventually it's just the empty screen left. It's the same with our lives – when all the stories finish, what's left is the pure, untouched essence of consciousness.

Here's another way to look at it—imagine the weather. Sunny days, stormy days, cloudy skies, gusty winds, droughts, famines, floods—they all come and go, right? And where do they happen? Within the atmosphere. At any given time perhaps all of those things are happening. They all take place in the space we call the atmosphere. Just as we discussed earlier, our feelings aren't telling us about our circumstances, our feelings are our internal weather report. It tells us what is happening inside of us.

We Are The Atmosphere

The finite mind usually feels *it is* the feelings, emotions, sensations, and perceptions happening "to it". The egoic mind might "wrap its head around these words and adopt the role of the passive observer, with a detached Zen persona. But, here's the thing, we're not just passive observers of the weather. We are the very atmosphere through which all these weather patterns unfold and are experienced. Take a moment to let that sink in. Imagine ourself as the atmosphere, with all the weather phenomena happening within us. What does just that fun little thought experiment do to shift our perspective slightly? Give it a try next time you experience a "negative feeling" merely to give yourself a novel experience.

Consider a cloud in the sky—it doesn't just pop up out of nowhere. It's constantly shifting and changing, influenced by the conditions throughout the entire atmosphere. Even though it may seem isolated, it's a manifestation of the entire system. So, just like the weather, everything we experience is not separate from us but arises within the vastness of our own being.

In the dance of our perceptual experience, we find a seamless interplay between what we conventionally label as objects and the field of awareness within which they arise. This distinction, however, is but a play of shadows upon the canvas of consciousness. Objects, sensations, and energies are all woven into the tapestry of experience, indivisible from the boundless expanse of awareness itself.

Why then do we persist in the delineation of separate entities? Allow me to offer a pointer, a concession to the limitations of language and concept. In attempting to articulate the ineffable, we find ourselves wrestling with the impossible task of describing the indescribable, explaining the unexplainable, and conceiving the inconceivable.

Yet amidst this linguistic dance, we encounter the undeniable simplicity of our true nature, effortlessly accessible and experienced. Reality reveals itself as a mysterious, ever-unfolding expanse—a field of consciousness, pulsating with infinite patterns of creation and dissolution.

But this simplicity often eludes us, obscured by the complexities of our conditioning. From an early age, we are indoctrinated into a worldview of separation—a narrative that paints us as isolated beings navigating a material universe of discrete objects and objective realities.

Yet, as we embark on the journey of self-inquiry, we begin to dismantle these illusions. We recognize that our experience defies the confines of separation, revealing a reality where subject and object dissolve into the seamless fabric of consciousness.

So, why then do we cling to our stories of separation? How do we stray so far from the truth of our own being? It is the seductive power of conditioning, woven deeply into the fabric of our cultural narratives, that perpetuates the illusion of separation. Perhaps.

Yet, through the light of awareness, we begin to unravel these illusions, returning to the simplicity of our true nature—the boundless expanse of consciousness, forever dancing in the rhythm of creation.

Chapter 5 Pulling the Veil of Illusion Over the Truth

"We can't solve problems by using the same kind of thinking we used when we created them."
~Albert Einstein

I love this quote from Einstein, he invites us to frequently shift perspectives as we encounter — "problems." Shifting Perspectives is something we do so effortlessly. We are sometimes fully mindful of the present moment. And, we can time travel back into our past, and forward into the future. When our mind is quiet and present, it is watching reality unfold Divinely. Sometimes we are rehashing memories or letting figments of our imagination run wild. Shifting perspectives is innate. In fact, it's kind of like our superpower.

Think about it: a busy exec might find herself mentally juggling work tasks while she's with her kids, or vice versa. Sure, it can distract us from the here and now, but this is also what drives innovation. Every invention, every big idea, starts as a thought.

Einstein nailed it when he talked about the mind being a faithful servant. But sometimes, we get stuck seeing everything as a nail because the only tool we know is a hammer.

Our society loves to paint things in black and white, good or bad, without appreciating the shades of gray in between. And that kind of thinking can blind us to the richness of reality.

It seems that awareness can easily get entangled in its own imagined constructs. The fleeting nature of experiences, coupled with our mind's penchant for seeking answers, often leads to skewed interpretations of reality. As we try to rationalize what's happening, awareness can contract, losing sight of its true nature amidst a maze of fabricated narratives.

This contraction of awareness, fueled by our tendency to identify with finite aspects of ourselves, makes it challenging to regain clarity. Once we start seeing ourselves as limited beings, it becomes difficult to perceive reality clearly, free from the veils of our own interpretations.

The more we buy into these mistaken views, the more confused we become. It's like the old saying goes, garbage in, garbage out. Our flawed understanding perpetuates further errors, leading to even greater confusion.

This is the predicament faced by many on the path of awakening. To break free from this illusion, one must first recognize the limitations of their understanding and be motivated to seek clarity. Only then can we begin to unravel the tangled web of our own making and perceive reality as it truly is, unclouded and unencumbered by our imaginary interpretations.

Bringing up this topic, I can't help but recall the profound symbolism in "The Matrix" movie. Remember that scene with the red pill and the blue pill? Neo is utterly bewildered, and Morpheus patiently guides him through the truth. Morpheus begins by likening Neo's experience to Alice tumbling down the rabbit hole. Neo responds, feeling a sense of surrender, expressing his desire to wake up from the illusion. Morpheus then delves deeper, probing Neo's beliefs about fate and control.

He uncovers something profound—Neo's innate sense that something isn't quite right with the world. It's a nagging feeling, like a splinter in the mind, leading him to seek answers. Though we want to overplay the metaphor, it's clear that the biggest obstacle to seeing reality as it is lies in our inherent disorientation, our entanglement in the dream.

Yet, amidst this confusion, there's a profound truth: consciousness, and awareness, always experience reality as it is, whether "we" comprehend it or not. This awareness serves as our greatest asset on the journey or realization.

Amidst the swirling confusion of our experience, there's an underlying current of consciousness—the very fabric of reality itself. Yet, at the heart of this confusion lies a fundamental misconception: the concept of separation, of individual entities existing independently.

As we've explored before, awareness reveals that nothing can truly be isolated from the whole. All aspects of experience arise and dissolve seamlessly within the field of awareness. However, it's this erroneous belief in separate existence that gives rise to elaborate fantasies of distinct worlds, multiple universes, and countless autonomous entities interacting according to imagined laws like causality and free will.

Once we entertain the notion of these entities as independently existing and enduring, we open the door to the possibility of their destruction. And thus, the stage is set for the illusion to perpetuate itself — the engine of separation fueling the illusion's persistence.

Fear acts as the engine propelling the train of illusion forward on its tracks. Instead of recognizing its true nature, the being immersed in the human experience begins to identify with the very entities it imagines. This identification leads to the next logical leap—that these imagined entities are vulnerable to destruction, whether it be through what we perceive as death or suffering.

This mistaken understanding gives rise to the powerful force of fear. When consciousness strongly identifies with aspects such as the psyche, ego, or the body, fear becomes a potent motivator to protect these imagined entities. This drive for protection often leads to the creation of what can be likened to psychological Rube Goldberg devices—complex mechanisms designed to achieve seemingly simple tasks.

For those unfamiliar, think back to the scene in "Back to the Future" where Doc Brown's kitchen is filled with contraptions intended to make breakfast, feed the dog, and more, but often failing to function as intended. Our psychological Rube Goldberg devices work similarly, often producing unintended consequences.

Here we encounter what the Buddha termed the Four Noble Truths—a profound insight into the nature of suffering. Simplifying his teachings, we suffer because we possess the faculty of imagination. Within this realm of imagination, we construct ideas and cling to their outcomes, thus birthing the emotion of suffering.

The Buddha's wisdom illuminates the prevalent worldview of humanity: our defense mechanisms, rooted in the ego's fabrications, grapple with a fundamental illusion. Like a mirage in the desert, these constructs appear substantial but lack true essence. Consider the shimmering lake on a hot horizon—a trick of light and heat, devoid of the water molecules that define a genuine lake.

Water, in its various states—solid, liquid, or vapor—remains fundamentally unchanged, composed of hydrogen and oxygen. A mirage, on the other hand, arises from heat and light, distinct from the essence of water.

Understanding this distinction offers a profound insight into the nature of reality. However, the challenge arises when we mistake the illusion for reality, constructing elaborate plans and actions based on its false existence.

In these scenarios, our efforts will inevitably fall short, leading to frustration, disappointment, and deeper confusion. However, from a spiritual perspective, this frustration can serve as a valuable ally in the journey of self-inquiry. It becomes a catalyst, motivating us to question the accuracy of our fantasies and assumptions.

This inquiry opens the door to a profound discovery: our mistaken beliefs are not true. It empowers us to unravel the fabric of illusion and uncover the true nature of reality. When awareness rests in clear, unobstructed experience, free from misinterpretations, we enter what some call the state of awakened awareness. For what we're truly experiencing is the natural, inherent condition of consciousness, continuously present and untouched by illusion.

The process of human domestication runs so deep that the state of awakened awareness often arises after a period of being enmeshed in illusion. When this clarity dawns, when awareness perceives unfiltered, unencumbered by conditioning, it's as if awareness has been liberated from the constraints of illusion, returning to its natural state.

Even amidst confusion, awareness remains unchanged—it simply experiences its own nature directly, functioning as it always has. The thinking, fantasizing, and conceptualizing about awareness are merely aspects of the illusion, not affecting its fundamental nature. As we grow to see reality as it is, we recognize whatever we add on top of reality is a constructed illusion. There is nothing wrong with the constructed illusion, nothing we need to do about it, nor is it anything we need to suppress. Once we understand the distinction of this true nature, we can bolt on conditioning on top of it, or not. For the sheer joy of it, either way.

Both our ability to imagine and our tendency to believe these imaginings as actual are functions of awareness. Just as a mirage is a real mirage, our imagined constructs hold a semblance of reality within the realm of awareness. However, when awareness rests in its awakened state, it perceives these imaginings for what they truly are—energetic manifestations of thought, devoid of the weight of conditioning or the stories we attach to them.

In this clear seeing, we recognize these manifestations as expressions of God's infinite love, consciousness, or awareness. Whether appearing as a friend, a lover, a cherished pet, or any other form, the world reveals itself as an expression of infinite beauty and pristine love.

Life unfolds before us, and we see it clearly for what it is—an expression of divine presence, manifesting in myriad forms, each imbued with the same essence of pure Being.

In embracing the present moment as it is, we invite in the pure essence of being—unfiltered, unbiased, unconditioned, dare I say, Unencumbered?

Even in the depths of confusion, the natural, unadulterated essence of awareness remains, happening effortlessly.

What we perceive as glimpses of liberation are, in truth, direct pathways to pure consciousness. Even confusion and illusions serve as vehicles for this unfolding. After all, what else could they be?

Recognizing this truth, we realize that the fundamental questions of the rational mind are distractions from the deeper reality. In disciplines like Neuro-Linguistic Programming, great emphasis is placed on the questions we ask, for they shape the answers we receive. When faced with unexpected news, the questions we pose reflect our conditioned identity. Asking "Why does this always happen to me?" reflects a limited perspective rooted in identification with the ego.

Let's consider the silver lining in what seems like a dark cloud. When faced with unexpected situations, the questions we ask ourselves can dramatically shift our perspective. Asking empowering questions opens the door to exploration, increasing the likelihood of receiving useful insights applicable to our current circumstances.

We're often conditioned to rapidly fire off a series of questions whenever something unexpected occurs. Now, imagine for a moment that we're living in the cabin where Henry David Thoreau once dwelled by Walden Pond. Although not isolated, Thoreau spent time contemplating existence and engaging with his surroundings.

Now, picture ourselves walking back to our cabin from the pub one evening. Suddenly, we hear a large being rustling through the woods nearby. This unexpected disturbance disrupts the tranquility of our surroundings. What unfolds in our mind in response to this noise?

Like Pavlov's dogs, we likely begin to run through a mental checklist, questioning what's happening and how to respond:

- What is happening?
- Why is this happening?
- What does this mean?
- Is this my fault?
- What should I do next?
- Am I safe?

The answers to these questions serve as the building blocks, shaping the ongoing narrative of "me." As individuals engage on their journey, it becomes apparent that these questions and the resulting personal narrative act as a veil over the deeper level of awareness—the pure awareness that lies beneath.

At the core of our being, our authentic self, or true self, remains unchanged. This level of awareness simply experiences itself spontaneously and directly, as it always has and always will.

Thoughts and emotions may arise, creating temporary ripples in the field of consciousness, but they eventually dissipate, returning to the vast expanse of awareness from which they emerged. This process unfolds continuously, day in and day out, shaping the ever-evolving story of our lives.

In recognition of our shared exploration, let us delve once more into the profound misconception that our thoughts are reflections of our circumstances. Consider when a thought arises and lingers, refusing to dissipate into the expansive openness of consciousness, but rather clings tenaciously like a persistent guest.

Think of it as akin to the wintry landscape described by Morpheus in "The Matrix" movie, where layers of rational inquiry cloak the mind: What is happening? Why? What does it signify? Am I to blame? With each layer, the narrow narrative sharpens, and we find ourselves ensnared in the web of personal identification, lost amidst the illusion of our thoughts sculpting our reality moment by moment. In that state, we are living the feeling of our thoughts taking form moment to moment.

Yet, if we pause and return to the grounded center of self-inquiry, we glimpse the truth: thoughts are but fleeting, insubstantial wisps arising within the vast expanse of awareness. They hold no inherent meaning, referring only to themselves, devoid of purpose or design. This recognition unravels the illusion of a separate self, dissolving the intricate layers of confusion that obscure the simplicity of being.

In the depths of meditative contemplation, we can witness the seamless interplay of energies within awareness, realizing that all phenomena emerge from the Divine essence of "I am." Through this direct experience, we unveil the falsehood of the superfluous narrative, liberating ourselves from the shackles of egoic constructs.

May we find equanimity in the experiential session that follows, as we journey together towards the boundless expanse of truth and liberation.

Chapter 6: The Pathless Path

You need not leave your room. Remain sitting at your table and listen. You need not even listen, simply wait, be quiet, still, and solitary. The world will freely offer itself to you to be unmasked, it has no choice, it will roll in ecstasy at your feet."

— Franz Kafka

Woven into the fabric of my memories is this quote. It's one of those sayings that just sticks with us, like an old friend we keep meeting again and again. I heard it the first time in '95, during this month-long meditation retreat. Picture me, diving deep into the TM Sidhis programs, seven years deep into my meditation journey.

But first, I need to rewind a bit, and we'll find me fresh out of college, itching to dive into the financial world. The problem was that the financial services industry wasn't exactly rolling out the welcome mat for me. Instead, they tossed me into the world of office equipment sales, as if that was my destiny.

I don't think I ever have run across a challenge I didn't believe I could win. My Mom was an amazing motivator with an unshakeable belief. She had this thing about believing in ourselves. If we can dream it and believe it, we can make it happen. She engraved it into my psyche. So there I was, armed with her mantra and a fierce work ethic, ready to conquer whatever lay ahead.

I wasn't exactly the life of the party back then. My nose was to the grindstone, determined to prove myself in the business world. I set a lot of goals and hit most of them. I was on a very traditional path, but despite having all the checkboxes ticked for success, there was this nagging feeling inside, like something was missing. Funny how life works though, isn't it? Through a series of serendipitous events – too many tangents to dive into here – I found myself signing up for a meditation class.

Two months earlier the thought had never crossed my mind, by the time the class was beginning, I didn't think anything was more important.

I threw myself into it, soaking up every bit of knowledge and technique like a sponge. As I delved deeper, my teacher noticed my earnestness and my dedication. So, they invited me into the TM Sidhis Program. Now, committing to this program wasn't a decision I took lightly. It was expensive, both financially and time-wise. I was already meditating twice a day for 20 minutes each, but this was a whole new level. Adding another 65 minutes on top of that – talk about a challenge for someone like me, always chasing goals and achievements. Where would I get the time?

Both meditation and the Sidhis Program offered glimpses of something profound, something beyond the surface level of existence. They gave me moments of Self-realization, moments where I felt like I was touching the essence of who I truly am. Sometimes it felt like I was sitting in God's lap. But those moments were fleeting. They felt like what I imagined enlightenment would feel like – if it was a constant undercurrent of bliss, this overwhelming sense of love pulsating through every fiber of my being.

Yet, I kept it all to myself. Partly because we were encouraged not to boast about our experiences – ego loves to jump in and hijack the narrative, after all. And partly because, well, how do we even put something like that into words? It's like trying to describe an orgasm to someone who's never felt one – it's ineffable. And deep down, there was this fear that maybe it wasn't real, that it was all just some illusion.

But regardless, those experiences stayed with me for days, lingering like the sweet aftertaste of a delicious meal, before gradually fading away into the background of everyday life.

The journey took me into the realms that members of the recovery community call chasing the dragon's tail – a poignant metaphor for the ceaseless pursuit of an ever-elusive high. I embodied that spirit in my own way, believing that if I just pushed a little harder, and worked a little longer, I could attain whatever I desired. And so, I found myself meditating three, even four times a day, chasing after that elusive dragon's tail.

Sometimes, amidst the quietude of meditation, I caught fleeting glimpses and tasted brief moments of transcendence. Yet, sometimes it felt like I was simply sitting there, on the cushion, chasing after an open secret. In the rational confines of my mind, conditioned by years of striving, the only solution seemed to be to sit longer and try harder. Little did I know then that my very approach was the stumbling block.

It took years of reflection to realize that those glimpses arose precisely because I approached meditation with a sense of openness, with no expectations, and no attachment to any particular outcome. It was in those moments of pure presence, unadorned by the trappings of desire or resistance, that I truly experienced the essence of Being.

The path, as I later understood, had no destination, nowhere to reach. There was no lack to be filled, no secrets to uncover. The only direction was the simplicity of being, here and now. Yet, for so long, I resisted embracing this truth. I believed I had to journey elsewhere and attain something more. It took years for the realization to sink in – that here, in this moment, is all there truly is.

Let that sink in for a moment: Here is all there really is.

Here, in the eternal now, is where we reside, where time dissolves into the infinite present. No matter where we journey, we'll find ourself here. It took time for me to grasp this fundamental truth, but once I did, it transformed my understanding of existence.

Allow the mantra to echo within:

Here is all *there* really *is.*

Feel the subtle shift in emphasis, the nuanced layers of truth encapsulated within these simple words. It's akin to a tale of old, of a kung fu aspirant journeying to the Shaolin Temple, seeking initiation into its sacred teachings.

In the muddy streets, amidst the rain, the novice is instructed to wait, to be present exactly where his feet touch the earth – a poignant lesson in the essence of now. It's reminiscent of my own journey, directed by brokerage firms to sell coffee machines before handling people's finances, each moment a test of the fire within.

DAYS PASS, AND QUESTIONS linger until the novice dares to ask the teacher: "How long until I become a true Shaolin monk?" The teacher, wise and measured, contemplates deeply before responding: "Fifteen years." Yet, the novice, driven by ambition, challenges the answer: "What if I devote every waking moment to the path? How long then?" Again, the teacher considers, then replies: "Twenty-five years."

"But master," pleads the novice, "I'll sacrifice sleep, dedicate twenty hours a day to my training!" The teacher, unmoved, gazes upon him with knowing eyes, offering a silent profound insight.

In the quietude of the temple courtyard, amidst the gentle patter of rain, the novice finds himself enveloped by the master's gaze in the embrace of Wu Wei, the principle of effortless action. With each droplet that kisses the earth, he learns a profound lesson in the art of non-doing. The Art of Being.

As he stands, rooted to the ground, the novice is reminded of the wisdom of nature. Just as the tree sways in harmony with the wind and the river effortlessly carves its path through the landscape, so too must he learn to flow with the currents of existence.

When he approaches the master with impatience and ambition, eager to hasten his journey to enlightenment, the master responds with a serene smile, embodying the essence of Wu Wei.

"Dear one," the master gently whispers, "the path to true understanding is not a race to be won or a goal to be reached through sheer force of will. It is a journey of surrender, a dance with the rhythm of life itself.

In our quest for speed and intensity, we risk losing sight of the delicate balance of yin and yang, of effort and ease. Instead of striving to accelerate time, we can allow ourselves to be carried by its gentle currents. Trust in the natural unfolding of our journey, and we will find that the universe conspires to support us in ways we could never have imagined.

Embrace the principle of Wu Wei, and we will discover that true progress arises not from frantic exertion, but from the effortless alignment of our actions with the flow of life. May we walk this path with grace and humility, attuned to the subtle rhythms of the universe."

In the quest along the pathless path, many have journeyed, their hearts aflame with earnest seeking. Yet, therein lies a paradox: the very act of seeking reveals the illusion of being lost. We are the love and happiness we seek. The only thing that keeps us from realizing that is we have yet to call off the search.

Glimpsing the truth in those early moments, felt like stumbling on a treasure, something precious that had been missing from life. And naturally, the tighter I clung the greater the fear of its loss. But here's the crux: my assumptions were flawed from the outset.

Consider the tale of our understanding of fundamental truths of the cosmos. Once, we believed the Earth to be the center of the universe, an assumption that led to countless adjustments to calendars and calculations. Yet, when Galileo dared to question this premise, suggesting that perhaps the sun, not the Earth, stood at the center, everything began to fall into place. But such insights were met with resistance, as history tells us.

Another example lies in the Black Plague, where our understanding of disease was clouded by misconceptions. We believed it spread through foul smells, leading to practices like carrying posies to ward off illness. But the truth was far removed from these superstitions.

In the same vein, the traditional idea of enlightenment can be likened to the ultimate goal, the pinnacle of spiritual attainment. Yet, perhaps therein lies the flaw – for in fixating on this goal, we may overlook the inherent truth of our being, already present in the here and now.

The idea that enlightenment is something to be obtained, and therefore there is a path which leads to its attainment, has birthed a vast industry of spiritual teachers, literature, and practices. Unfortunately, many fall into the trap of believing that to attain enlightenment, one must alter their thinking.

These teachers offer a myriad of prescriptions for changing our thoughts, feelings, and behaviors, promising that once these adjustments are made, we'll effortlessly embody the state of no self, embodying the divine and shedding all limitations. These supposed solutions range from cultivating compassion to learning to vibrate at specific frequencies, or clearing our closets of trauma via shadow work.

This narrative plays seamlessly into our conditioning of self-doubt and inadequacy. We've been indoctrinated to believe that we're flawed and in need of constant improvement. So naturally, we cling to these promises of transformation, willing to surrender our autonomy and resources in pursuit of this elusive goal.

In reflecting on my journey, I've come to realize that while I pursued various practices and ideas in search of enlightenment, I now see that the destination I sought was never separate from me. There's a profound truth here: the path we travel and the destination we reach are one and the same.

Upon closer examination, one might notice that these spiritual frameworks often evolve into self-perpetuating social structures. They begin to prioritize sustaining the organization over the genuine pursuit of self-realization. This begs the question: what if we already possess what we seek? What if there's no external pot of gold waiting at the end of the rainbow? {By the way: the rainbow is an illusion. A trick of the light. The trick is real, and the illusion is real, it's just the rainbow is not.}

The crux of the matter lies in understanding that we are already the essence of what we yearn for. Our perceived separation is merely a misunderstanding rooted in the natural play of consciousness. When this is recognized, the cycle of confusion is broken, revealing the inherent perfection of our true nature.

Let's delve a bit deeper into this notion of confusion from a traditional perspective.

In the traditional view, confusion often appears to stem from external circumstances, reflected in our emotions and feelings. However, when examined from a deeper perspective, we realize that emotions primarily reflect our internal state, not external events. So, when confusion arises, it's not necessarily a sign of chaos in our surroundings, but rather a signal about the state of our inner landscape.

Consider confusion as a messenger urging us to gather more information, seek clarity, or deepen our understanding. Rather than being overwhelmed by it, we can approach confusion with curiosity, seeing it as an opportunity for growth and insight.

We may wonder, how does awareness facilitate this transition from confusion to clarity? The beautiful truth is that awareness, in its innate nature, is clarity, serenity, tranquility, and equanimity. We, Awareness, do not need to force or manipulate anything; all unfolds effortlessly, motivated by the intrinsic intelligence of consciousness itself.

Reflecting on my own journey, I recall moments when clarity dawned not through striving or effort, but through a simple act of letting go. In those moments, there was no goal, no attachment to a desired outcome. It was a surrender into the pure state of being, free from the entanglements of Maya, the illusion that veils our true nature.

Think of any A-ha moment. We are frustrated by a vexing problem. Finally, we hear wisdom whispering we need a break.

It's crucial to recognize that the process of awakening isn't about frantic activity or endless seeking. Rather, it's about allowing awareness to recognize its own essence, to untangle itself from the web of social conditioning and egoic patterns. While engaging in various activities may seem to play a role in the apparent journey, true awakening unfolds naturally, gradually dissolving the egoic mind until it merges seamlessly with the boundless expanse of consciousness.

So, as we continue on our apparent path, remember that we're already endowed with all the necessary grace and fortune, it is who we are. Whether we're on the brink of awakening or navigating through moments of utter confusion, realize whether we trust in the inherent intelligence of consciousness to guide us home or don't think of it at all. What we are seeking is seeking us. When we realize that we will realize the only rational step is to call off the search.

Unencumbered - Chapter Seven
Seriously? Is that all you've got?

If the voice inside your head asked that question at the end of the last chapter, recognize we're in very good company. Many folks, including your author and narrator, have heard that question asked by the inner critic upon first being exposed to this concept. Rather than beginning this chapter with a quote, what I would rather do is start with a story from these traditions.

The story is called "The Seeker and the Sage."

ONCE UPON A TIME, IN a distant land, there lived a seeker whose name was Kabir. Kabir dwelled on top of a mountain and was known throughout the land for his profound understanding of the inner workings of life and the universe. Having become obsessed with the quest for enlightenment, Kabir asked everybody that he came across whom he should talk to and where he should go. He studied tirelessly, seeking guidance repeatedly. He was told that the wise sage lived atop Kailash mountain. So, Kabir embarked on a long and arduous journey to reach the sage's home at the top of the mountain.

The journey took many months, and finally, Kabir arrived at the foot of the majestic mountain. He climbed with determination, overcoming challenges and obstacles along the way, until he finally reached the sage's humble dwelling. With great reverence, he bowed before the sage and asked, "Wise sage, I've traveled far and wide seeking the path to enlightenment, the path to awakening, the path to truth. Please tell me, Master, what is the path that I must follow?"

The sage looked at Kabir, his eyes wide with great surprise, and replied, "My dear seeker, you have indeed come a long way. I must tell you that there is no specific path that you must follow." Kabir's eyes widened in disbelief, and he said, "Wait, what? No! You don't understand. I traveled so far in search of your wisdom!"

The sage smiled gently and replied, "I understand your journey, my friend. But awakening is not a well-trodden road that can be mapped out. There are no particular signposts or mileposts along the way, no GPS coordinates that you can plug into your smartphone to guide you. There are no steps to follow, no gates to pass through on the pathless path."

Needless to say, this was not good news for Kabir. He felt a mix of confusion and disappointment. "Well then, how can I find enlightenment? How can I find awakening? How can I reach that truth that I seek?"

The Guru's eyes twinkled with amusement. After a chuckle, the sage spoke again, "My dear seeker, self-realization is not something to be found externally. It is already within us, woven into the fabric of our being. We need not seek it outside of ourself. In fact, it is that very conditioned impulse to look outside that seemingly makes this journey so difficult. Instead, let us turn our gaze inward, quiet our mind, and listen to the whispers of wisdom that flow 24/7 from our heart."

Kabir was taken aback. "How do I do that? How do I listen to my heart?" The sage laughed again, his belly shaking like a bowl full of jelly. "My dear seeker, it is not about 'how'; it's about 'being.' Let go of your need for the prescribed path. Embrace the silence, the stillness, and the present moment. In that space, you will discover the truth that has been patiently waiting within you."

Kabir pondered the sage's words. Although he had hoped for and expected a more straightforward answer, he realized that the sage's message carried a deeper meaning, one that he was likely going to need to sit with a little while longer. On that realization, he bowed once more to the sage and expressed his gratitude for the wisdom that had been shared.

As Kabir ascended the mountain, he carried the sage's teachings with him. Over time, he learned to let go of his fixation on the predefined path and embrace the beauty of the present moment. Through this, he learned to let go of his preconceived ideas of what this experience may look like. In the end, he let go of the need to resist or insist on any part of the process. Bit by bit, different aspects of his true, authentic self emerged as he awakened to his true nature. And in time, through revelation, Kabir began to share the sage's timeless tale, reminding all who heard it that the path to truth, to awakening, to self-realization, is not a road to travel but an inner journey of self-discovery that transcends external boundaries. Transcends time and dates, it is a pathless path during which you will travel through a gateless gate and come to explore the depths of our own heart.

If you are hearing any pushback after listening to this part of the message, after experiencing this part of the journey so far, I want you to become intimately familiar with the voice that's speaking to you right now.

Recognize it for what it is - the voice of the inner critic, of our conditioning, of the rational mind - the faithful servant-doing mind. It's that part of the mind that asks critical questions:

What's happening?

Why is this happening?

What does it mean?

Is this my fault?

What should I do?

Am I safe?

Now, odds are good that we're probably already familiar with this voice of the inner critic, the voice of the finite doing mind because, for many people, this voice is prevalent 24 hours a day, seven days a week, every day of existence. This is the mind that we try - and as I say that, I'm using this word in a very ironic sense because there is no "try". Yet this is the voice that we "try" to silence during meditation. If you've ever tried to silence that voice, one thing you've probably noticed is the more you try to shut it up, the more it feels like it's yapping on incessantly. One of the challenges is that we think *that's our voice, those are our thoughts.* Let's explore that and see if this idea holds any water.

An experienced meditator, who frequently or at least occasionally experiences a very deep level of silence, a deep level of inner peace, extended periods where the inner critic simply isn't weighing in, will tell us that the pathway to that deep silence is literally doing nothing - not engaging with the thoughts, not paying attention to the thoughts, not assisting or resisting the thoughts. Because anyone who's ever tried to stop thinking will resonate deeply with the first line of that very popular adage: "What we resist will persist."

As we learn to silence the voice of the inner critic - not really silence it because that implies a certain action - it would be better stated to say that as we release the need to engage with the voice of the inner critic, that voice naturally and effortlessly fades into the background. Suddenly, we become aware of another voice. This is the voice of the intuitive mind, our intuition. It's the voice of our gut. It is the voice of our inner guru, which also speaks to us 24/7. But rather than the voice of judgment or ways to make things even better, it's the voice of wisdom.

And here's the thing: the voice of wisdom speaks in whispers. If we find ourselves in a situation where our constant companion is chronic mental stress, mental static, if the chatter of the inner critic is this relentless cacophony of noise, it's fairly difficult to hear the whispers of wisdom.

Pondered the paradox of these two voices: the loud one that speaks in English or whatever happens to be our native tongue, versus the whispers of wisdom that speak more in symbols, ideas, metaphors, feelings, and emotions— not so much in words. It's almost like learning a new language. But the good news is, it is our language. It is our innate language.

One of the biggest challenges lies in the human domestication process. We're taught to condition our awareness to play well and be functioning members of society. In doing so, we often condition out those whispers of wisdom. Because at some point along the way, when we're in control as we are parent to child, we're a lot more interested in compliance than in helping our charges discover their truth. Just think about the message that's actually being sent.

There are fairly common phrases that are well-known, well-worn, contain some wisdom, and are useful at many times. But they're like that preferred real hammer in our toolbox: if it's our only tool, and we tend to walk the world looking for a nail. Here are some of these phrases:

- "No pain, no gain."
- "Suck it up and power through."
- "It's not how often we get knocked down, it's how often we get up again."
- "Embrace the challenge."
- "Push through the discomfort."
- "Face hardship head-on."
- "Rise above the obstacles."
- "Stay strong in adversity."
- "We have to weather the storm to see the rainbow."
- "Grind now, shine later."
- "Keep your eye on the prize."
- "Don't back down, stand your ground."
- "Don't give in, give it your all."

Now, there is wisdom in these sayings, for sure. However, what they're telling us is to ignore the pain in the moment for some supposed reward that is going to come at some point in time. Is it any wonder that our conditioned route to awakening often includes the idea that it needs to be a struggle? Because we're conditioned to believe that the greater the struggle, the greater the reward, the greater prize in the end? Man, we love a good underdog story. And there's nothing wrong with those stories— up until the point that it's the only story left to tell ourself.

I wrote an article a while back called "Reimagining the Cherokee Parable of the Two Wolves." This parable in its original form and found this adaptation useful for guiding people along this ride. If you're not familiar with the original parable, let me share it with you: A Cherokee elder is teaching his grandson about life. He tells his grandson, "A fight is going on inside of me. It's a terrible fight. It's between two wolves. One is evil. He's anger, sorrow, regret, greed, arrogance, self-pity, guilt, resentment, inferiority, lies, false pride, superiority, and ego. And the other wolf is good," the elder continued talking to his grandson. "He is joy, peace, love, hope, serenity, humility, kindness, benevolence, empathy, generosity, truth, compassion, and faith. And that same fight is going on inside of us and every other person," the elder said to his grandson. The grandson thought about it for just a minute and then asked his grandfather, "Which wolf will win?" And the older Cherokee simply replied, "The one we feed."

While I love this story on many levels and appreciate how it honors native wisdom and the love of a grandfather for his grandson, it misses the mark just a little bit. It indicates that this elder is lost in the illusion of our perceived reality. So, back in 2021, while looking for something to do in the middle of COVID, I decided it was time to revisit this piece of ancient wisdom. This time approaching it from the perspective of self-realization.

You might be wondering, does it miss the mark? This parable pits good versus evil. As Joseph Campbell pointed out in "The Hero with a Thousand Faces," tales of good and evil are nearly as old as our facility with language. We love the hero's journey, and these intricately woven stories are knitted into the fabric of the human experience.

The mind, the rational mind, loves. It loves to write and create hierarchies. The mind is on constant guard to keep us within the limited set it perceives for itself. It wants to keep us safe, and it perceives danger around every corner. The mind views so-called negative emotions as evil emotions that are to be avoided. The mind finds these tales fascinating, magnetically attractive, and even irresistible.

Now, on revisiting this tale from the point of view of awakeness, being, Christ Consciousness, Soul, or exemplifying God's infinite love, we realize that what we are witnessing is the hypnosis of social conditioning in action. The grandfather, simply and innocently, elegantly demonstrates this.

Through this parable, he reinforces the illusion of separation. He encourages the boy to buy into this perceived reality, to identify with his mind and not his true self. It's a conditioned tradition handed down from generation to generation.

To paraphrase Einstein, the mind is an invaluable tool and faithful servant. Wisdom is our true, authentic self and Our Sacred gift. The hypnosis of social conditioning trains us to worship that servant and ignore Our Sacred Gift, ignore our birthright.

From the point of view of our true, authentic self, from our point of view of awakened awareness, from our point of view of our Divine I Am, our Soul, no emotion is inherently good or bad. It's just information.

An easy analogy to demonstrate this idea is the gauges on the dashboard of our car. If we walk outside and start our car and notice that our fuel gauge is pegged to the right, indicating it's full, the mind will instantly think that's good. Maybe it is unless we've spent our last dollars to fill it up and it's a week until payday. In which case, maybe not. If we're about to drive three miles to the grocery store and back amid the next pandemic lockdown, a full tank of gas could easily be irrelevant. But a conditioned mind will reflexively point out "however," the mind still loves and has one less thing to worry about. And it frees the mind up to look for others.

That's good. Maybe, maybe, unless we spend our last dollars to fill it up and it's a week until payday. In which case, maybe not. If we're about to drive three miles to the grocery store and back during the next pandemic lockdown, a full tank of gas could easily be irrelevant, but a conditioned mind however, still loves it. That's one less thing to worry about. And it frees the mind up to look for other phenomena.

If we are driving 80 miles an hour? Is that inherently good or bad? Well, it depends completely on the context. If we're running late and the speeding is allowing us to arrive on time for an important interview, and the police are distracted elsewhere doing crowd control for mostly peaceful protests that are taking place downtown, then that could be good. If we're driving the Seward Highway here in Alaska on a foggy night, very, very bad.

Conditioning tells us our "negative" emotions are to be avoided. Ask almost anybody what their idea of enlightenment is, and one of the things we're likely to hear is, "I'll never experience a negative emotion again; blue skies and sunshine 24/7."

Sure, mention a negative emotion to somebody else, and we're likely to be told, "Man, you need to just lock that down for the time being. We need to power through this; you can just suck it up and snap out of it." It's like "no pain, no gain" is just the mantra for those happily and robotically wandering through the illusion.

The idea of noticing that our car is on fumes if we've got a big drive ahead of us and having some intense Tony Robbins-style "success coach" telling us to power through is somewhere between absurd and the beginning of a funny SNL skit. For younger readers, SNL is the weekly sketch show that used to be very funny. And yeah, yeah, I know, yet another "Boomer" talking about the good old days.

Why, then, are we berated into ignoring the whispers of wisdom guiding us lovingly, gently, and effortlessly through the human experience?

So, in revisiting that parable, I'd like to make just a couple of adjustments for a more enlightened age, or an awake and aware age, and see if this newer version might serve as a pointer away from the illusion back to the space within, back home again.

The Parable of the Two Voices:

A CHEROKEE ELDER IS teaching his grandsons about his authentic spirit. "Two conversations are going on inside of me," he said to the boy. "It's a battle for attention, and it's between two voices.

"One is loud and incessant. This voice is critical. It preaches lack; it tells me that I'm not good enough. It tells me that I will only be happier with a prettier young squaw, a bigger tepee, a sharper knife, and a faster horse. It tells me I need more eagle feathers for my headdress, and I don't get to save the ones that I've already earned.

"The other one whispers. It tells me I'm part of all that is part of all that will ever be, the great nature. It tells me that I am one with the buffalo, the elk, and the beaver. It tells me when I kill the elk, I'm strengthening the herd. When we follow the geese before the corn moon to winter in the deep valley, we feed the crows and ravens with what remains of our abundant crops. This one tells me that the Great Spirit asks only that we live in harmony with the guidance and wisdom that is older than life itself. It tells me our true nature is joy, peace, love, serenity, and kindness. Generosity, truth, compassion, and faith.

"This same fight is going on inside of you, grandson, and inside every other person too." The grandson thought for a minute and then he asked his grandfather, "Which voice will win?" The old Cherokee simply replied, "The one we heed."

These so-called negative emotions—how would our life unfold differently if we didn't mistakenly consider them to be engaged in telling us about our life's circumstances?

We need only pull the thread of those emotions to notice there is a way we want our life to unfold, a way that apparently we need our life to unfold. And the world is not complying with our desires. This is the clinging to attachment that the Buddha realized was the cause of all suffering.

Perhaps another example will help illustrate this particular point. Let me give you two scenarios.

Scenario One: A man gets off the plane and checks the departures to see which gate his final flight to Miami is going to be leaving from—C 25. But the flight's delayed, no ETA. He realizes there's a pretty high likelihood now that he's going to miss his best friend's engagement party. Not surprisingly, anger arises. He storms off to the Customer Service Desk, demanding answers. No info is available; {otherwise, his flight info would have been updated on the screen}. He makes a scene, he screams at the gate agent, and he's asked to step away by security. He heads to the bar, needing a drink. He orders a gin with a chaser of self-loathing and frustration. His mind steps in, reminding him that he had the option to fly out last night. His inner critic regales him with a list of other times when he was less than a stellar friend. And the self-loathing continues until an alcohol-fueled downward spiral ensues.

Scenario Two is both similar and completely different. A man gets on an airplane and checks the departures to see which gate his final flight to Miami is leaving from—C 25. But the flight is delayed, no ETA. He's probably missing his best friend's engagement party. Anger arises—very different from the normal blissful state that he normally experiences. He considers what this means and recognizes that it's a signal that he's attached to a map, to an imaginary unfolding of a life different from the one that's playing out. He uses the grounding technique of his choice to get centered and aligned. He calls his best friend to let him know that he's delayed, then heads off to a bar to catch the last three innings of the Marlins game. At the bar, someone catches his eye, and then he catches hers. She twirls her hair, and suddenly, adventure is afoot.

Now, the initial facts of these scenarios are identical. What's different is the vastly different reactions. Because of this vast difference in their reactions, it shows us that the feelings they experience have nothing at all to do with their circumstances. It's only indicative of their internal experience, their access to resources, and their grounding. In other words, it's like a fuel gauge or a speedometer. It's information—neither inherently good nor bad.

For the self-realized being who chooses to approach life as a perpetual meditation each day, the way we make our way through the human experience, a very simple mantra can mean merely noticing which voice we're listening to.

The inner critic, for whom the squaw is never pretty enough, for whom the tepee is never big enough, and for whom the knife is never sharp enough.

Or

Are we showing up as this Great Spirit? One with the elk, the buffalo, and the beaver, guided by wisdom in harmony with nature.

Having served as a guide for hundreds of seekers, in what for them has been the pathless path to the end of seeking, I can suggest at its essence, it is no more difficult than the binary check-in:

- Are we showing up seeking love? Are we showing up as love?

- Are we acting and reacting from the egoic body-mind or from the Divine I am?

- Are we responding from a scared place or a sacred space?

"Course Correcting" can be as simple as knowing that we are alive and suddenly realizing and remembering that we are the light. Once this awareness has arisen, it's simply flipping the switch.

If you've ever read A Course in Miracles, you may be familiar with the phrase with which they begin the book:

"Nothing real can be threatened. Nothing unreal exists. Here lies the peace of God."

IF YOU'VE READ THAT book even just a little bit, you know what they're talking about. When they refer to the peace of God, it's that state that we commonly call Christ Consciousness, awake awareness, pure consciousness, pure being, Buddha nature, the Soul, the Divine I Am.

What that phrase and that story are pointing toward is that which is infinite and eternal—the authentic self.

It is an invitation to simply realize that when we identify with the body and we believe the body is us when we believe that the mind is us, we're heeding that First Voice. That's the voice of the trickster, the voice of the illusion, the voice of a con man.

For the conditioned, rational mind, being told "We don't need your help" is like the worst thing that it could hear. And it will push back. With the several hundred people that are taken individually through this process, I would say half or more have at some point said some version of, "So what am I just supposed to meditate, not do anything at all?" Or they might say, "So what am I supposed to just not try or just not care?"

That's not the message. The truth of the matter is, in a post-self-realized state, we are going to be more aware, more in tune, and we're probably going to care more. We'll just be less attached to the specific outcome. It will be less important that life unfolds specifically as it was imagined.

I took a class on cartooning one time, and the very first lesson of the class was just randomly making any sort of shape, scribbling anything on the paper, crumpling it up, and tossing it over our shoulder.

Again and again,

Throughout the entirety of first class, that's all we did: mark up the paper, not giving a crap about what the design looked like, crumpling it up, tossing it, and grabbing another blank page. It was an exercise in embracing the "abundance mentality". It was an exercise leading to the embodied realization that there is no failure, only feedback.

I'll give you a couple of examples. If you've ever grown anything in the garden, you know there's not very much for you to do. We've got to dig the hole, we can make sure that the soil is nutrient-rich, put the plant in there, and loosen up the roots if it's been growing in a pot for a little bit, so those roots are freed and unencumbered. Then just water it and stay out of the way. Nature doesn't need our assistance, it doesn't need our resistance; the wisdom of the universe, the natural intelligence has our back.

If we're cooking rice, the conditioned rational mind wants to lift the lid and see how it's doing; it wants to stir the pot. But all we've got to do is Google "cooking rice," and we'll see that stirring the rice while it cooks is something that we never want to do because every time we lift the lid, we're letting the steam out. We're lowering the temperature of the pot. The result of lifting that lid may end up undercooking our rice or cooking it unevenly. Also, our rice doesn't need to be stirred while it's cooking. Stirring the rice while we're cooking is going to break up the grain, and we're going to end up having a pot of unappetizing gruel.

Perhaps the best analogy of all is learning how to ride a bike. Riding a bike is something that we cannot learn from reading. We have to learn by doing because the key to being able to ride a bike is learning to "be one with gravity". We're not conquering gravity; gravity is still there. It's acting specifically and consistently. The concept of "conquering gravity" makes no intellectual sense. We're learning to be in harmony with gravity.

To steer the bike, we have to lean, and we ride gravity like we ride a wave. The process of learning how to ride a bike is one of trial and error. We have to feel our way into it. We have to listen to the wisdom that's telling we how much is too much and how much is not quite enough. Initially, we try to exert dominion over nature but it has never worked. Once we have learned to relax into harmony with nature, it suddenly becomes effortless and we could peddle our way around the world.

It's one of those things that once we learn it, we tend to never forget it. In fact, we use that as an analogy. It's like riding a bike. Once we got it, we got it.

Now, in each of those examples, there are things we can do to help out the process. With the plants in our garden, we can till the soil, fertilize it, make sure that it's getting good water, or maybe add some specific nutrients that will aid in the growing process. We can test the soil to find out what it's lacking and maybe make those adjustments along the way. But never are we going to dig the plants up to check the roots and see how they are doing.

When it comes to the rice, we can use good cookware, and make sure that we've got a stove that's distributing heat equally and efficiently. We can make sure that our water is pure, measure the amount of water that we're adding, and the amount of rice that we're adding so that we have the optimal blend to tilt the scales as much as possible toward success.

My favorite one, possibly because of my age, is the bike analogy. It's been around 60 years since I learned how to ride a bike. Back in the day, the way that we did it was we bought the bike with pedals and we put on training wheels, and we learned how to ride the bike. Then we introduced gravity in there and lifted those training wheels just a little bit so that we can begin to play around and harmonize with gravity, but do it in a completely safe way.

That's the way I learned, so as conditioning often dictates, that is the way my kids learned. My son was a little bit reluctant to take the training wheels off, that is until one day I followed him around the block, and his training wheels never touched the ground. I was able to say to him, "You already know how to ride a bike. You just did it, and you just did it perfectly."

Now, as I get to the age where I might start having grandkids, I see other little kids that are learning how to ride a bike, and I notice two things: one is they're learning a lot younger and they're learning using a better tool. They're learning now on balance bikes, no pedals, feet flat on the ground. And the ease and effortlessness into the realization that we already know how to interact harmoniously with gravity, having walked the pathless path myself through the gateless gate.

Having been along for the ride and served as a guide for hundreds of people who have been on this journey, I can tell you that this journey is much easier if we think of it as an undoing, as an unlearning. Don't think of it as something that we've got to add. There are not a bunch of practices that we need to pursue. There are no new mantras or mudras that we need to learn. Rather, we simply need to relax into what already is, and our biggest challenge is going to be our conditioning.

They say that it takes 10,000 hours to master a new skill. I don't know if that's right or wrong or not, but it seems to be well accepted {which we might have realized only makes it common, doesn't make it "right"}. Check this out, here's the thing: by the time we reach the age of majority, by the time we're 18 years old, social scientists tell us we've got 25,000 hours of training and instruction, 25,000 hours of indoctrination into the human experience. The keeper of all of those rules is our constructed self, our identity. That's the container that all of our values, all of our beliefs, all of our best practices. The container that they're held in is what we commonly call the ego or our constructed identity. That's the voice of the inner critic. But the whispers of wisdom have a different story to tell.

And one of the holiest books in the Hindu tradition is called "The Bhagavad Gita". The story takes place in a conversation between Lord Krishna and Arjuna, and it takes place on a battlefield. Lord Krishna is Arjuna's charioteer; he is his servant. The story was reimagined by Steven Pressfield in the book "The Legend of Bagger Vance." Also, the story of a battle, but in the story of Bagger Vance, the battlefield is a golf tournament. And Lord Krishna, or the Bhagavan, is Bagger Vance, Arjuna in the book is Randolph Junuh or R Junuh.

There's a beautiful dialogue in the middle of it that I'd like to share with you. The scene is Matt Damon is having a perfectly awful day. He plays the golfer, Randolph Junuh {"Arjuna" in the story}. Bagger Vance, played by Will Smith, is his caddy. At one point, the caddy says to the golfer, "I think it's time for you to see the field."

The field in this metaphor is the truth. The field is consciousness. The field is awareness. The field is our true, authentic self. As Bagger Vance gets ready to show Matt Damon the field, he says, "Put your eye on Bobby Jones over there. It's like he's searching for something {and then he finds it}. Now watch how he settles himself right there in the middle of it. Feel it. He's got a lot of shots that he could choose from—slices, tops, duffs, and skulls. Only one shot is in perfect harmony with the field—one authentic shot. And that shot is going to choose him. There's a perfect shot out there trying to find each and every one of us, Junuh. All we've got to do is to get ourselves out of the way, to let it choose us.

You can't see that flag as some dragon that you've got to slay. You've got to look at it with soft eyes. See that place where the tides and the seas and the turning of the earth all come together. Where everything that is becomes one. You've got to seek that place with your Soul, Junah. Seek it with your hands. Don't think about it, feel it! Our hands are wiser than our head is ever going to be."

Then he says, "Now, I can't take you there. I just have to hope that you find your way. Just you have that ball, and that flag, and all that you are".

This is true of our journey as well."

It's like when Neo and Morpheus are walking down the hallway on the way to see the Oracle, and Neo says to Morpheus, "I know what you're trying to do." Morpheus waits a little bit to hear what he has to say. In response to hearing nothing, Morpheus says, "I'm trying to free your mind, Neo, but I can only show you the door. You have to walk through it."

This too is true of our journey. The rest of this book will be experiences, pointers, and aphorisms all pointing toward the door, all pointing toward the field, all pointing to our true, authentic way. So, I'll say, "Ciao" for now, until we reconnect in this chapter's audio.

Chapter Eight:
"The Finger Pointing at the Moon."

For the most part, this chapter will consist of a series of pointers—just some ideas, experiences, and opportunities for a deeper exploration from perhaps a slightly different angle than we've approached before. It might give us a glimpse into a deeper layer as we delve into intimacy. Like peeling back the layers of an onion, we're uncovering conditioning that has been placed on us since we were two years old.

This message could be called the teaching that doesn't need to be taught or the teaching that has always existed. Many of the great Masters have said that there are many teachers, but fundamentally there is only one message. We've been exploring the idea that there are no teachers, no teaching, just this message.

This message isn't meant to replace anything. Not other teachings you may be familiar with pursuing, or any religious concepts or doctrines we follow. Many report it deepens those experiences, while others sometimes see those concepts dissolve, neither is the goal of this message.

For some, it can deepen those teachings. For some, it might replace them with a more direct experience, but that's not the goal. Throughout this, we'll explore how others have expressed this message. We are talking about something that can't easily be put into words, so for no reason in particular, we explore even more words.

We mentioned before that the great anthropologist Margaret Mead noted that there has never been a society that developed without an understanding of a higher power or natural intelligence.

If we assume this is true, this means every person who has walked this planet has felt this realization. This message is about wholeness, liberation, and love. On some level can we say, that common to every religion and spiritual tradition that has arisen spontaneously is that at its core, pointing toward wholeness, freedom, and liberation from the ties that bind us and keep us separate?

A Course in Miracles teaches us that in every moment, every day, we are either showing up from one of two states of Being: As Love or Seeking Love.

We are showing up as awareness, as being, or we're showing up lost in the illusion of separation. The Seeker or the Essence.

As the seeker, we're lost in the illusion because, in those moments, we're seeking love. As we come to the embodied understanding we are Love, the only sensible response is to call off the search.

This message is, simply, that We are Love. To paraphrase Lao Tzu, the love that we can describe or put into words is not the love we are discussing. We are talking about Love that is unconditioned, infinite, and eternal.

The ultimate goal of any spiritual pursuits, practices like meditation, contemplation, contemplative prayer, devotion, purification rituals, and even more esoteric pursuits involving fasting, hallucinogens, or ecstatic breathwork or movement; all are attempting to find the center of our authentic selves, pure awareness. To create a space and a context so that everything that has been blocking us from seeing this will dissolve.

There comes a moment when love, peace, and joy become the new normal. Anything else becomes a pattern interrupt that grabs our attention, prompting us to pause and check in with ourselves. To explore the inner landscape.

When we show up as the Divine I am, these triggers become catalysts for self-inquiry. Allowing us to reclaim and rein in conditioned responses.

If we find ourselves lost in illusion, no reason to "beat ourselves up" the mere realization, the mere "finding ourselves" will serve as guidance from Source. As we become present, this realization brings us home. We don't need to "do" anything. The wholeness in this message, the Oneness of all that is, becomes so obvious, that it can only ever be momentarily overlooked or noticed.

In this chapter, we'll explore the way others have shared this message. Many voices are delivering this message, and for whatever reason, some voices resonate more. There may be a point where listening to this message becomes quite enjoyable, other times, not so much. Just listen, we have the ears to hear.

I invite you to explore with the understanding we are hearing messages through our conditioned filters right up to the point we are not. As we notice these filters explore them. Perhaps one teaching expresses this message in a way that resonates most with our conditioning. If some of these teachings seem particularly beautiful, go with that. Allow that resonance to guide us. If some seem off-putting, question whether there's something in our conditioning that's making it sticky for us. Thoughts are repetitive; we have thousands every day. It's time to break free from that cycle.

Most thoughts come and go, following the advice of one of these teachers, Shunryū Suzuki, a Zen master who implored us to open our hearts, open our minds, open the front door and the back door, and allow thoughts, feelings, and sensations to come and go freely. Just don't serve them tea. Don't engage with them. Recognize them for what they are—appearances in consciousness.

So, this message can become a pointer, a rumble strip on the highway of life. When we notice that thoughts are coming and going, appearing and disappearing, recognize them as ephemeral, transient, and temporary. This is awareness. This is us showing up. This is as it is.

It can be lovely to merely witness what is arising as awareness, no judgments, no right or wrong, without any preferences. Ultimately, there won't even be those; those will ultimately collapse as well.

We might momentarily engage with them. However rather than becoming lost back in the illusion, riding the energy playing with it as energy for the sheer joy of doing it. Unbounded, Unencumbered, Unconditioned energy we can label anything we want, having an experience.

Other times we fall completely asleep again. Completely identified with our thoughts, feelings, and perceptions. Perhaps we will fall back into the belief we are separate beings, we'll stay there as long as we do and it might occur this can be a good opportunity for exploration.

These rumble strips of life that I'm talking about, to go back and explore and ask yourself, "What's going on? There will be a high likelihood that this will lead to agitation. We will likely very soon, or perhaps we already have realized this is always the case with these "so-called" negative feelings. We will notice when we are resting in Pure Being, these feelings are absent. The State of Pure Being is the absence of everything except Love.

Therefore, Wondering why is this getting under my skin? Why does this seem to be agitating me?" This is an excellent question to ask, for the answer leads only to one non-local destination, home.

The second messenger is Nisargadatta Maharaj. Pronouncing his name is an effort...right until the moment that it isn't anymore.

Wisdom is knowing I am nothing, Love is knowing I am everything, and between these two my life moves.

So wisdom says that I am nothing, that the idea of self is nothing but an illusion. I am awareness. I have no center, I have no moment in time, no location in space. I exist, but I exist in a place where non-locality prevails. Love says that I am everything. What a difference in the way that life unfolds when we are showing up as love rather than showing up seeking love.

"Love thy neighbor as thyself, wholly and completely," and between those two, my life flows, meaning that sometimes even living in this realization, we may feel very much like a person, we may get lost in the illusion, we may lose our temper from time to time. The difference is that those will now become pattern interrupts. An invitation to return home to the space within, or if that doesn't occur it will become a catalyst for self-inquiry. Of going within to explore where our conditioning is still affecting us. Other times, we are going to feel like divine love, or we're going to feel like emptiness, and we're going to look out at the world, look at nature, look at the city, look at its people, and we're going to see nothing but love, nothing but unbounded energy.

We'll see love flowing in the waterfall, we'll recognize ourselves in the grumpy cashier or bank teller, we'll laugh at the aspect of getting angry with something that is nothing more than another aspect of the Divine, a reflection of ourselves, a contraction of the infinite and eternal.

This is Bliss.

You are no doubt familiar with what is commonly called the yin/yang symbol. It is synonymous with kung fu and is in the center of the Korean flag. Typically black on one side, white on the other, but with a dot on the other. We call it the yin/yang symbol in the West, but that's not its name; its name is Taijitu. The symbol is made of two aspects. When we draw it we begin with a circle. This is the first aspect. Wuji {or Wu Chi} is the infinite emptiness. Wuji is consciousness, and Wuji is awareness as we have been describing it.

This is the space inside of which everything occurs. These occurrences provide variety and uniqueness, allow for preferences, and allow the experience of good and evil. It is the space within which everything is experienced, through which everything is known and explored. As we explore preferences, one can have what seems good and seems bad, but as we explore those, we notice that we only notice the big through the small, we only know the good through the evil and the evil through the good, we only know that after follows before, and this is the Taijitu.

This is the blending, this is the entanglement of all those objects that we talked about in one of the meditations that we recently went through. It reminds us that the apparent separateness is a mirage.

Explore the concept of what is big. Big is only known through something small. A basketball is large compared to a ping pong ball, but a basketball is minuscule compared to the earth.

As the world of relative preferences becomes a signal to come back to awareness, an interesting opportunity arises as this begins to look more and more like a lucid dream.

Let's play with an idea for a moment.

Lucid dreaming is a phenomenon that occurs during the REM (Rapid Eye Movement) stage of sleep when we become aware that we are dreaming while still in the dream.

This awareness allows the dreamer to exert some level of control over their dream and the events that occur within it.

Often while dreaming, we are so wrapped up and identified with the dream, that it seems real on every level. We have amazing experiences in the theater of our imagination, then we "wake up". As we awaken, there is a sense we are leaving one "state of consciousness" and entering another. We have agreed to call this awake and asleep. Our conditioning tells us this is true, and likely is beginning to wonder when we get to the point.

What if this is a mirage? What if we are still dreaming? A shift has merely occurred from "REM" dreaming to lucid dreaming. "You" just control the dreamer. "You" control the characters in the dream.

If this makes sense, then we are seeing exactly what we have been pointing to and working toward. We are controlling the character in the dream. We are the awake awareness inside of which this dream is occurring. This is happening by us and for us. This as it is, is made of us. The character writing these words and the character reading these words are the same, everything we see, feel, hear, touch, taste, and sense, all our experiences, all our emotions

It feels like when we "wake up", we have entered "another state of consciousness. Just called awake or up. We have been conditioned to believe when we are awake, the sleep is over, and the dream is over.

What evidence do we have that is true? I have never found any, and I have spent quite some time looking. Have you?

Go check right now, can we find any evidence that we are not just in the lucid part of the dream right now?

We are experiencing the state of mind we call "awake", we all agreed at the meeting and that is what we call it. Yet, just consider this, if I am lucid dreaming, and I am dreaming of you, while you are lucid dreaming, and dreaming of me, how cool would it be to be able to interact with our friends, our lover{s}, our parents and our children while we are still dreaming, but dreaming lucidly while they are too, to meet in the dream and play.

As we play with this idea, it begins to simply make more sense. From the perspective of this realization, as we consider the idea that we are the dreamers, suddenly the idea of awakening doesn't feel far-fetched at all, does it?

As we sit with it just a little bit longer, it simply occurs the reason it doesn't seem far-fetched is it has become obvious. It's been there all along. That's why we call it the elusive obvious.

And as we realize we are seeing it now, let that saying *"Once we've seen it, we can't unsee it"*. Just sink in and resonate. Let it resonate that we have no desire to ever unsee this.

We are the dreamer {The Spiritual Being} having the dream {The human experience}. The dream is occurring in us, it is of us, it is by us.

So this is it. This is the realization which changes everything and nothing.

Let's just sit with this idea for a minute.

Does it feel like you are being asked to believe something right now?

If it does, just see it for what it is, what is the idea you are being asked to believe? Got it?

Now let's just sit with it for a minute, seeing this for exactly what it is...it's an idea, arising in us, right now.

Let's just sit here with it for a moment. Just get clear on it as it arises.

Sit with it for a moment more.

See it as it is. It is an idea arising, it doesn't need to be right or wrong, and it doesn't need to have any meaning at all. Sit with that a bit more.

Does it have to mean something? What happens if we permit it to mean nothing at all? How does it feel realizing we are the one who gives the permission?

Now revoke that permission and either assign it a meaning or let it pick the meaning it would like to have.

Sit with the idea for a moment that we are the ones that give the permission, or withhold the permission, or let the whole concept called permission simply dissolve.

Notice the lightness and clarity that becomes unencumbered from the former ideas and concepts, what we might simply call "things", that these arisings meant something.

Feel the liberation, realizing we are source. Everything, absolutely everything, thoughts, feelings, ideas, concepts, sensations, perceptions, beliefs, values, and objects arise in awareness.

We have never known anything outside awareness, for to know it is to be aware of it, which is simply another way of saying "it's occurring in awareness".

Check that out, whatever is arising in us right now, what happens if we don't choose to assign any meaning to it at all?

What happens as we consider it has no inherent meaning? It just is.

And yet we have the freedom and the power to assign any meaning to it at all.

Recognizing this power, notice what meaning occurs when we just ask what it means. Now just for fun, let it mean the opposite of that and just see how it feels to take that idea for a test drive.

Notice the feeling of space created by the expansion of space inside of which we are working.

Revisit this at will. This program will prove useful for attuning our Inner GPS. GPS is Grounded in Profound Stillness. It is from this place we will uncover the ears to hear the whispers of wisdom.

And just enjoy the paradox of the statement This changes everything and nothing.

It changes everything as we realize "everything" is all the concepts, sensations, thoughts, ideas, perceptions, and all the apparent objects. We might never look at them the same way again.

And it changes nothing. This is excellent because ultimately we come to understand...

NOTHING NEEDS TO CHANGE.

Have fun playing with this.

There is a quote that I love from the Bhagavad Gita, and the quote says, "There is neither creation nor destruction, neither destiny nor free will, neither past nor achievement. This Space is the final truth."

So, if we look at that a little bit, it encapsulates a very profound teaching from this revered text in the Advaita Vedanta tradition of India. This philosophy emphasizes the non-dual nature of reality, which asserts that there is ultimately no fundamental distinction between Atman and Brahma, between the individual self and the ultimate reality.

Let's break down different aspects of this quote and explore their meaning within the context of this teaching. First, there is no creation or destruction. This challenges the traditional idea of a beginning, a middle, and an end; the illusion of birth, life, and death. We see these as separate processes, but from the non-dual perspective, the ultimate reality is beyond all dualities. Existence exists before manifestation. It suggests that creation and destruction are not inherent properties of the ultimate reality, but rather perceptions within the realm of relative existence.

The second part is that there is neither destiny or free will. This addresses the apparent conflict between determinism and free will. This non-dual view transcends this duality by pointing out that both destiny (what we would consider fate or preordained events) and free will (individual agency) are concepts that pertain to and are part of the realm of duality. Once again, this is a pointer that we are slipping back into our conditioning.

The third part is there is neither past nor achievement. This speaks to the idea of spiritual paths and goals, and even grand goals like enlightenment. The quote suggests that the ultimate truth does not require a specific path, and does not require prescribed achievements. This doesn't negate the value of spiritual practices in any way but underscores that the final realization is not a product of effort. It's not something that we achieve or attain; it is merely the recognition of what already is.

The Bhagavad Gita is one of the holiest books in the Advaita Vedanta tradition, Advaita which means "not two". Vedanta refers to the Vedas as all of the stories of the Hindu pantheon of gods. The Vedas are long songs and poems to be memorized. "Anta" means the end of. So Advaita Vedanta means, Not two, the end of the vedas.

It means even more than that as some is lost in translation. They don't say one because that implies an object with form. There are not the two of duality, an object nor a subject. It represents the formless, the void, from which form is manifested.

One of the pointers that we've mentioned more than once is this idea of neti, neti, or the neti neti process. This is often translated as "not this." It's a fundamental concept and a technique used in the practice of self-inquiry and meditation within various traditions and philosophies, especially Advaita Vedanta and various schools of yoga as well. It is a process that is important to transcend the limitations of conceptual thinking, to transcend the limitations of our conditioning, and ultimately to arrive at the direct experience of the true nature of reality or the true nature of God's infinite love or Christ consciousness.

Let's start with the idea of transcending conceptual limitations. The process of neti, neti involves negating as a means of surpassing and creating liberation from the limitations of language and thought, from transcending the limiting beliefs and worn-out mental models, and the hypnosis of social conditioning. When we identify something as just a conditioned response that we had, we say "okay, It's not that".

It might embody this process if you have a junk drawer and you need to find something in the junk drawer. You know your checkbook is located there; you haven't used a check in years; you used to have a checkbook lying around somewhere, and suddenly the need arises to write a check. So, you delve into the junk drawer, and you start pulling out tools, cards, birthday gifts, balls of string, and balls of rubber bands, and you just set those aside because you're looking for the checkbook. Anything that's not the checkbook, for expediency, you can simply say, "That's not it. That's not it. That's not it," and just create a new pile until ultimately, the checkbook is revealed. This is the same way that we use the neti, neti process to reveal our true, authentic being, the essential isness.

The ultimate goal of this is the revelation of our unchanging self. As the seeker systematically negates all aspects of experience, they arrive at a point of recognition where all that can be negated is discarded, and what remains unchanged is the unchanging self.

This is the blending, this is the entanglement of all those objects that we talked about in one of the previous meditations. It reminds us that the apparent separateness is an illusion because what is. This big?

Well, big is only known in relation to something small. A basketball is large compared to a ping pong ball and all that.

As we enter the world of relative preferences, that can be a signal to us that we are slipping our way back into the illusion. Strong preferences arise from conditioning, so as we feel ourself becoming attached, notice and create the space and agency to return home via GPS Grounded Private Sanctuary. From here a conscious desire to embody the role and feel the preferences, completely choosing to lose ourself in them.

Another well-known pointer that is worthy of our exploration is a very common Zen saying. Other people on a spiritual path all the time are likely you've heard it, and that saying is, "The finger pointing at the moon is not the moon."

This is not the end. If you've been on any type of spiritual journey for any length of time, you've heard this, and it encapsulates a very important truth and message. It encapsulates the idea that while the message and all the words and all of this exploration might seem to serve as valuable guides. They are not the ultimate truth.

The emphasis is on transcending these conceptual understandings, moving to direct experience, the direct experience of the truth that lies beyond the words and the concept and beyond conceptualization is a very important ideal in Zen philosophy.

There is a recognition that language and concepts are limited in their ability to capture the fullness of reality. We've talked about that with sunsets and chocolate and orgasms. This thing underscores that truth, which is often referred to as suchness or emptiness, or isn't it so being is that something that transcends the boundaries of language was there before the conceptual understanding of language was even understood that the truth can only be grasped through direct experience, unfiltered by the constraints of conceptual thinking.

The very reason that this book is an audiobook is because I wanted to be able to give us these experiential, contemplative guided visualizations so we could have the direct experience.

The next one that I'd like to explore is known as The Heart Sutra, one of the most revered and concise texts from the tradition of Mahayana Buddhism. This teaching encapsulates profound insights into the nature of reality, the relationship between form and formlessness or emptiness, and it is the essence of non-dual understanding. "Form is emptiness, emptiness is form." So, let's look deeper:

The Heart Sutra

Thich Nhat Hanh translation

Avalokiteshvara

while practicing deeply with

the Insight that Brings Us to the Other Shore,

suddenly discovered that

all of the five Skandhas are equally empty,

and with this realisation

he overcame all Ill-being.

"Listen Sariputra,

this Body itself is Emptiness

and Emptiness itself is this Body.

This Body is not other than Emptiness

and Emptiness is not other than this Body.

The same is true of Feelings,

Perceptions, Mental Formations,

and Consciousness.

"Listen Sariputra,

all phenomena bear the mark of Emptiness;

their true nature is the nature of

no Birth no Death,

no Being no Non-being,

no Defilement no Purity,
no Increasing no Decreasing.
"That is why in Emptiness,
Body, Feelings, Perceptions,
Mental Formations and Consciousness
are not separate self entities.
The Eighteen Realms of Phenomena
which are the six Sense Organs,
the six Sense Objects,
and the six Consciousnesses
are also not separate self entities.
The Twelve Links of Interdependent Arising
and their Extinction
are also not separate self entities.
Ill-being, the Causes of Ill-being,
the End of Ill-being, the Path,
insight and attainment,
are also not separate self entities.
Whoever can see this
no longer needs anything to attain.
Bodhisattvas who practice
the Insight that Brings Us to the Other Shore
see no more obstacles in their mind,
and because there
are no more obstacles in their mind,
they can overcome all fear,
destroy all wrong perceptions
and realize Perfect Nirvana.
"All Buddhas in the past, present and future
by practicing
the Insight that Brings Us to the Other Shore
are all capable of attaining

Authentic and Perfect Enlightenment.
"Therefore Sariputra,
it should be known that
the Insight that Brings Us to the Other Shore
is a Great Mantra,
the most illuminating mantra,
the highest mantra,
a mantra beyond compare,
the True Wisdom that has the power
to put an end to all kinds of suffering.
Therefore let us proclaim
a mantra to praise
the Insight that Brings Us to the Other Shore.
Gate, Gate, Paragate, Parasamgate, Bodhi Svaha!
Gate, Gate, Paragate, Parasamgate, Bodhi Svaha!
Gate, Gate, Paragate, Parasamgate, Bodhi Svaha!"

THIS IS A STORY THAT echoes across ages, whispered by sages and scholars to their adepts for centuries. Now with technology, it is accessible to such a broader audience. A sacred script known as the Heart Sutra.

Why this name?

Open your heart, Listen closely, for within its verses lies the very essence of Mahayana Buddhist wisdom, the heart of a great journey.

At the heart of this sutra stands Avalokiteshvara, a bodhisattva of boundless compassion, his presence a beacon of love amidst the vastness of emptiness. You see, dear explorer, the Heart Sutra isn't just about voids and negations, but about the embrace of compassion within the emptiness.

Picture it like this: a garden, barren and desolate, yet within it blooms a single flower, radiant with warmth and kindness. That flower is Avalokiteshvara {Ah-VAH-lo-kah-TESH-varah}, reminding us that even in the vast expanse of emptiness, compassion blossoms eternally.

But beware, for without a tender heart, the journey through emptiness becomes a desolate path. Emptiness without compassion is like a sky without stars, a landscape devoid of life. Thus, before we embark upon the study of this sacred text, we must first cultivate the soil of our hearts, nurturing compassion within.

Now, let me share a secret with you. Within the Heart Sutra lies an invitation, an invitation to release our burdens and surrender to the flow of existence. Imagine, if we will, replacing every "no" in the sutra with the burdens that weigh upon our soul: "no fear," "no pain," "no sorrow." Suddenly, the words take on a new depth, resonating with the struggles of our own lives.

As we journey through the Heart Sutra, let us not merely recite its verses, but let us delve deep into our hearts, exploring the emptiness within and embracing the compassion that fills it. For in this sacred journey lies the true essence of wisdom, a wisdom that transcends words and touches the very core of our being.

In Buddhism, form refers to the physical and phenomenal world, the illusion or perception, appearances, and concepts. Emptiness, on the other hand, does not refer to void or nothingness but rather to the fundamental reality, that Wuji mentioned earlier in the yin-yang diagram, the unconditioned, that which is beyond conceptual limitations.

The profound interdependence and non-separation of these seemingly distinct concepts teach us that form and emptiness are not two separate or opposing realities but rather two sides of the same coin. All forms and phenomena arise from and are inseparable from the very nature of emptiness itself. The formless is the Source of all forms.

The Heart Sutra teaches us to move beyond dualistic thinking and to focus more on the Wuji. This teaching transcends dualism, which tends to perceive the world as a series of objects, hierarchies, good and evil, or at the very least, good and bad. By stating that "Form is emptiness and emptiness is form," the sutra invites us to move beyond these dualities, to perceive the underlying unity of all.

The Way that can be spoken is not The Eternal Way.

The next teaching comes from the Tao Te Ching by Lao Tzu. I have quoted the opening verse of that many times. The opening line is "The Tao that can be told is not the Eternal Tao." This profound statement encapsulates the essence of Taoist philosophy and spirituality.

This line emphasizes the ineffable, transcendent nature of the Tao, of life, of the ways, and the underlying principles that shape and sustain the universe. Lao Tzu invites us to challenge the limitations of language. Diving instead into direct experience. In that tradition, it simply means living and embodying the Tao. This is considered a 'mystical' approach in Western thought.

The perceived reality we live in is linguistically structured, and becoming very good with language can help in understanding this perception. However, the Tao is not something that can be fully captured by language. It cannot be confined to words, and any attempt to define or explain it falls short because the Tao exists beyond the realm of human language. The Tao invites us to surrender to its ungraspable nature.

The Tao, often translated as "the way," represents the fundamental order and flow of life and the universe, encompassing both the seen and the unseen, the known and the unknown. By stating that the Tao cannot be told, Lao Tzu implies that it's not a subject to be comprehended, nor an object to be held. It transcends the boundaries of human understanding, creating what is known as the paradox.

The Tao Te Ching frequently uses paradoxical language in its expression, aiming to convey its teachings by pointing towards experience and away from intellectual understanding.

In the Christian tradition, there is much discussion about the idea of wholeness, oneness, and unity. A statement attributed to Jesus, "I and My Father are one," found in the Gospel of John (John 10:30), carries deep theological and spiritual significance within the Christian tradition, reinforcing broader unity teachings.

This statement is often interpreted as reflecting the unity between Jesus and God the Father. When combined with another statement from the Bible (John 14:12), where Jesus says, "Truly, Very truly I tell you, whoever believes in me can do the works that I have been doing and they will do even greater things than these because I am returning to the Father,". This suggests that the same Divine essence within Jesus is also within every individual. This echoes the idea present in many spiritual traditions that the ultimate reality transcends the distinction between self and other. This also echoes my experience.

Throughout history, many Christians have reported mystical experiences where the boundary between the perceived individual self and the Divine dissolves, often referred to as miracles, leading to a profound sense of unity. Jesus's statement reflects a mystical insight into his identity as the Son of God and his deep awareness of unity with the Divine Source.

Another significant verse from the Christian tradition is Psalm 46:10, which encapsulates profound spiritual insight, encouraging a contemplative and inward approach to connecting with the divine. The verse, "Be still and know that I am God," resonates with the essence of these teachings by emphasizing the importance of stillness, inner awareness, and direct experience with the Divine Presence. This invitation to stillness encourages quieting the mind, silencing thoughts, and entering a state of profound inner stillness, a fundamental practice found in almost every spiritual tradition in various forms.

It has to do with knowing from direct experience, "Be still and know that I am God." This points to a form of knowing that goes beyond intellectual understanding. All of the traditions we've noticed this theme; they go beyond intellectual understanding. This is a way of reminding us that the moment that we stop and rationalize wanting to create a story or want to wrap our minds around these concepts, it's telling us that we're getting off track. The finite mind, the rational mind, is incapable of understanding the infinite. As the physicist Niels Bohr once said, "Reality is not only stranger than we think it is, it is stranger than we can imagine."

The last one that we'll explore in this particular audio is one that you've no doubt heard before, and I think in many ways, is one of the most important sayings. So we'll explore this one a little bit more deeply than we have some of the others, and that is the Zen saying, "Before enlightenment, chop wood and carry water; after enlightenment, chop wood and carry water." According to legend, this was the response that the Buddha had to one of his disciples who was anxious and fired up about achieving Satori, awakening, enlightenment, and realization. They wanted to know what it was like, how they would recognize it when it happened, and what they could expect when this happened. This goes to the idea that enlightenment is this grand thing, that once it happens, it's going to be nothing but blue skies and sunshine, and we're never going to get angry again, never going to experience fear, never going to suffer again. We're going to transcend all of those ideas, and we've built it into this massive achievement that many of us don't even believe that we have the right to expect, at least not necessarily in this lifetime.

This phrase, "chop wood, carry water," encapsulates the idea of integration of spiritual insight and ordinary, everyday life. The saying highlights the continuity of our daily activities before and after awakening or realization, emphasizing that even after this profound awakening, the practical aspects of life don't fundamentally change.

Let's explore that a little bit more deeply. We'll begin with the idea that there's an emphasis on the ordinary. The mind wants to blow up this concept of enlightenment into this grand thing, this life-changing experience. Some teachers have said some version of the idea of enlightenment as it is commonly spoken of in everyday language is the ultimate job for the ego. Should somebody just declare themselves to be "enlightened"? The ego to jump on and say, "I've got this. Do you want to be enlightened? I know how to play Enlightenment." But it's not a role; rather, with the same, emphasizing the ordinary. The saying underscores the importance of everyday activity in the context of the spiritual journey. "Chopping wood and carrying water" just represent the basic tasks that are essential for our everyday survival in the human experience. They symbolize the routine tasks and responsibilities that make up a lot of the human experience. It also delves into the paradox of continuity, the repetition of the phrase "chop wood, carry water" before and after.

Enlightenment points to this paradox. On one level, it's suggested that there is a sense of continuity in daily life regardless of one's spiritual state. The message is even more profound. A profound spiritual insight doesn't exempt the individual from participating in the mundane world. As I have shared this teaching with various individuals over the past 7 years, one of the common responses is, "So what, I'm gonna get this, and then I'm just gonna sit and meditate?" That's where we're going with the "chop wood, carry water" – that we're still going to be doing this but now we're going to be integrating the profound and the mundane.

This saying that comes from the Zen tradition emphasizes the integration of spiritual realization with the mundane aspects of life. It speaks against the notion that awakening or realization or enlightenment leads to some sort of complete departure from worldly responsibilities. Instead, it teaches that true awakening involves fully engaging in the world and the experience and the illusion while maintaining the profound awareness of unity and God's infinite love, bliss, joy, and happiness.

It talks about living in the present moment. The same encourages individuals to live in the present moment, regardless of their current emotional or mental state. Chopping wood and carrying water requires attention, presence, and mindfulness. This aligns with the emphasis on being fully engaged with the moment, no matter what the activity – that is at the heart of mindfulness. It also deals with the illusion of change. The same challenges the idea that external circumstances need to change for someone's experience to be transformed. While awakening brings about this deep inner shift, the external world remains largely unchanged. This emphasizes that true transformation occurs on the inside, within the individual's perception and understanding. In essence, the saying "Before enlightenment, chop wood, carry water; after enlightenment, chop wood and carry water" conveys the idea that the journey of spiritual growth does not remove us from the responsibilities of daily existence; rather, it encourages us toward the integration of these profound insights into the fabric of ordinary life. The saying reminds us that the way that we engage with simple tasks and simple responsibilities, can be transformed by a very deep understanding of the connectedness, the interconnectedness, to the unity of all.

Oh, I know I said that would be the last one, but I gotta do one more. And this one comes from Buddha. The Buddha said, "There is no path to happiness. Happiness is a path." This teaching encapsulates the profound insight into the nature of happiness and the pursuit of well-being. Is that what we are seeking?

The fact that we are seeking is the very reason that we're not experiencing it now because we perceive it to be something that is outside of us. The same highlights a perspective that challenges some of the concepts about the pursuit of happiness. So let's expand on that teaching just a little bit. We can look first at the idea that we're talking about transcending external attachments and in conditioned thinking, people often believe that happiness is something to be pursued. We've talked about that before.

All conditioning revolves around the idea that you are not currently enough, but if you add ABC or XYZ or LMNOP to you, you get the new you.

You + LMNOP = YOU 2.0

This tension challenges this idea by suggesting that happiness is not dependent on external factors. It looks like our feelings are telling us about our circumstances, but they're not, not ever, not once.

So instead of seeking happiness as a distant goal to be attained, the Buddha invites individuals to recognize that happiness is not something that we will acquire; rather, it is an inherent intrinsic aspect of who we are.

It also introduces the idea that the journey is the reward, and the saying simply implies that happiness is not a destination that is reached by a specific path, but instead, this process of experiencing life itself as it is; is where happiness is found. The moment that life as it is; is the path and by fully engaging in every moment, the essence of Zen, the essence of mindfulness, the essence of non-duality, one can uncover the inherent joy that exists within every experience.

Happiness isn't found by constantly striving for a better future or dwelling in the records of the past, but rather by being fully present and engaged in the moment. One can discover contentment and fulfillment that arises naturally from the awareness of the present moment. It also points to this idea of inner tranceformation, and the teachings of Buddhism often emphasize the importance of inner-transformation, the cultivation of qualities like compassion, wisdom, and mindfulness.

Cultivated even is a curious word. These aspects of our selves don't need to be cultivated; rather, they need to be revealed. By pulling on these threads and peeling back layers of the intimacy onion, becoming very intimate with ourselves, and by letting go of attachments and desires, individuals can uncover a deeper sense of well-being that's not contingent on external circumstances.

Of course, all Buddhist teachings get back to this idea of non-attachment. The teachings of Buddhism are rooted in the principle of non-attachment. This reinforces the idea that true happiness is not bound by attachments to transient things, but rather by letting go of attachments we allow the experience to be a more enduring and profound experience of joy that is everlasting and not subjected to the fluctuations of the ups and downs of the human experience.

These teachings challenge the notion that happiness exists outside of us and must be captured or pursued; or that it can be "obtained". Experientially understanding the nature of this paradox, allows us to soften our eyes and see. Looking through the prism the Buddhists call "Beginner's Mind".

This invites individuals to embark on an inner journey of self-discovery, of mindfulness, and transformation. This realization is that happiness is not a distinct goal, not a way of living or being, rather the essence of who we are..

These can all lead to a more profound and sustainable sense of well-being: love, bliss, joy, resilience, compassion, and everything else that we've been conditioned to believe is something worthy of achieving. We're simply saying here that it is part of the original equipment installed at the factory by the manufacturer.

So these are teachings from various traditions that reinforce this universal idea of unity and unity is a universal idea, but conditioning makes it seem like it's something magical that happens, something extraordinary.

These teachings are merely pointing us to the idea that they are the exact opposite. They are not extraordinary. They are extremely ordinary.

Well, I hope you've enjoyed this review. I think both this audio and this chapter might serve as a resource we can go back to again and again.

As you revisit these from time to time, you might notice that they get a little bit deeper. As you go deeper, these teachings get deeper.

In fact, it could be said that the only difference between this class which this book, we could call the introductory teachings, and what might be considered at some point as advanced teaching the only difference between the basic and the advanced is in the advanced, the listening, and the perceiving are a little bit deeper.

The End!
La Fin!

Al Nihaya!

El Final!
Das Ende

Ka Hopena!

An Deireadh!

El Fin!

About the Author

Robert "Bobby" Cobb, acclaimed Financial Advisor turned transformative peak-perfromance coach, is a pioneer in the realms of human potential. Known for his tireless pursuit of excellence and unyielding dedication to empowering others, Cobb's journey from financial success to inner fulfillment is nothing short of extraordinary.

With a career marked by accolades and achievements, Bobby's quest for transformation led him to explore the depths of Neuro-Linguistic Programming (NLP) and hypnosis, ultimately culminating in the development of his groundbreaking Outer Game protocols. However, it was a pivotal moment during a mastermind session with his top clients that ignited a profound shift in Bobby's focus, propelling him toward the exploration of the "Inner Game" and our authentic relationship with self.

In a radical departure from conventional hypnosis, Cobb's mission transformed from inducing slumber to awakening individuals from the trance of societal conditioning. His own transformative Realization

Experience in 2017 served as the catalyst for the birth of "Triaspecta: 3 Aspects of Experience" and the revolutionary Liberation Hypnosis protocols. Through a multifaceted approach encompassing books, podcasts, videos, and classes, Cobb shares his message of liberation—unveiling the inherent wisdom within and guiding others toward a life unencumbered by illusion.

Described as "fiercely reductive," Bobby challenges the prevailing narrative of self-help formulas, advocating for a profound shift from a paradigm of lack and fear to one of abundance and authenticity. His teachings echo the timeless wisdom of sages, emphasizing the innate divinity within each individual and the boundless potential of living in alignment with the whispers of wisdom.

Bobby Cobb's work stands as a testament to the transformative power of self-discovery and the profound liberation found within the depths of one's own being. Through his unparalleled guidance, readers and listeners are invited to embark on a journey toward the realization that the Kingdom of Heaven lies not beyond, but within.

Read more at www.tranceformativechange.com.

www.ingramcontent.com/pod-product-compliance
Lightning Source LLC
Chambersburg PA
CBHW051847130726
47987CB00002B/720